The Book of
Jewish Practice

The Book of Jewish Practice

Louis Jacobs

BEHRMAN HOUSE, INC., PUBLISHERS
West Orange, New Jersey

A companion volume to:
THE BOOK OF JEWISH BELIEF

PROJECT EDITORS: Arthur Kurzweil and Nicolas D. Mandelkern
PHOTO RESEARCH: Naomi Patz

Published by Behrman House, Inc.
235 Watchung Ave., West Orange, NJ
MANUFACTURED IN THE UNITED STATES OF AMERICA

Library of Congress Cataloging-in-Publication Data

Jacobs, Louis.
  The book of Jewish practice.
  Includes index.
  1. Judaism—Customs and practices. I. Title.
BM700.J35 1987   296.7′4   87-14559
ISBN 0-87441-460-1

For my grandson

Michael Zvi

Contents

The Book of
Jewish Practice

Belief in Action

A Religious Way of Life

The phrase "belief in action" has a double meaning: first, that Judaism believes in the high value of an *active* religious and ethical life; and second, that Jewish belief must find its expression in deeds.

Beliefs are extremely important. Activity, even of a religious nature, is mechanical and lifeless unless based on sound convictions. Judaism, as a religious way of life, requires of its adherents that everything they do be grounded in faith. Jews believe that when they do what Judaism expects them to do they are carrying out the will of God. Yet to hold true beliefs without translating them into concrete deeds is to be at odds with the Jewish way of life.

An example may be found in the observation of the Sabbath. It is one thing to declare a belief in God as Creator of the universe, but quite another to give this belief actual expression by observing the Sabbath—by refraining from labor and by performing positive actions such as reciting the *Kiddush* and carrying out other Sabbath rituals. It is the translation of the belief into the vocabulary of practical deeds that constitutes a vital religious outlook. It has been said that the difference between religion and philosophy is that religion "does something about it." Judaism believes in doing something about it.

Moreover, there is, Judaism maintains, a right and a wrong way of doing things. It is obvious that there are varying degrees of observance among Jews today (perhaps it has always been so). Some try to keep all the laws in all their details. Others set lower standards for themselves, strict in some matters, far less scrupulous in others. Others, again, may choose to limit their observances to the home or to special days like Rosh Hashanah, Yom Kippur, and Passover. For all that, there has generally been a desire, among Jews, when they do choose to follow the law, to do whatever has to be done in the proper manner. (Perhaps this tendency explains the astonishing popularity of digests of Jewish law.) It is far from unknown for a Jew to say, "I may not put on *tefillin* every day, but if and when I do decide to put them on I want to do it correctly." Or a Jew may declare, "While at the moment I am not too fussy about keeping the dietary laws, I do want to know what is involved in keeping kosher in case I eventually decide to have a kosher home." From the point of view of strict adherence to the law, such picking and choosing is not tolerated, yet the reality of the situation is that many Jews are selective in their practice and wish to be informed how to observe, with authenticity, whatever they select.

Jewish tradition calls for precision, reflecting its view that there is a right way and a wrong way of doing things.

Judaism is not just a philosophy or a point of view. It is a call to action: Don't just sit there, do something about it!

Action Reinforcing Belief

Judaism places the emphasis on the deed not only as a necessary consequence of true belief but, more significantly, because belief itself becomes more firmly engrained when it is put to work in the deed. A belief in God, for instance, is hardly present in the mind of even the most devout all or most of the time. By giving expression to belief in God through the various rituals, the belief itself becomes lodged in the mind and heart to inspire further action, which, in turn, fortifies belief. Practical Judaism is of the essence.

This idea, of action reinforcing belief, is behind all Jewish observance. Two simple illustrations may here be given. The tremendous theme of Passover, that God has redeemed His people from slavery to be free persons owing ultimate allegiance to no other than God Himself, could have been reflected on by reading books about the Exodus and in praise of freedom. But Judaism has a better way of getting the message across—through eating *matzah* and avoiding *ḥametz*; through celebrating the Seder with the Haggadah, the bitter herbs, the four cups of wine, the hymns, poems, and melodies. It is by these concrete means—tangible, earthy, and robust—that the deeper impression is made and earth is brought a little nearer to Heaven. That is why the Passover rituals are still required even if we think we already know it all, or as the passage in the Haggadah has it, "Even if we are all wise, even if we are all persons of rich discernment, even if we are all knowledgeable in the Torah."

The second illustration is from the rules about blessings. The Jew who, when drinking wine, recites: "Blessed art Thou, O Lord our God, King of the universe, Creator of the fruit of the vine," has a constant reminder of how pervasive are God's gifts and His wonders in nature: He knows that God wishes His creatures to enjoy His marvelous world in which there is growth and abundance and joy. To utter the right words is also to carry out a deed. The verbal formulation allows vague thoughts to emerge in a way that gives body to them.

"To hold true beliefs without translating them into concrete deeds is to be at odds with the Jewish way of life."

Repeated Actions

Maimonides is so convinced of the power of repeated actions to influence character that he advises a person who has a large sum of money to give to charity not all at once, but a little each day until the whole sum has been given. His argument is that a magnificent act of benevolence may be the result of a momentary impulse without lasting impression. Steady giving, on the other hand, promotes increasing benevolent feelings as these are exercised time and again even when the mood is absent, resulting in an eventual transformation of character. It is not only the mood that promotes the deed. The deed, regularly performed, helps effectively to create the mood.

Translating creed into deed: the Jewish community of Budapest operates a van bringing hot meals and eggs to the elderly.

Approaching Observance

A story is told of Franz Rozenzweig, the influential German-Jewish theologian, who grew up in an assimilated home but became increasingly observant as he got older. One day an acquaintance asked him if he put on *tefillin* every morning.

"Not yet," Rozenzweig replied.

As long as the answer is "not yet," Jewish practice remains a possibility. With time, with effort, and with an open heart and mind, a Jew might yet return to a life of tradition and *mitzvot*.

This book seeks to provide a clear account of the correct manner of carrying out Jewish practices. There are chapters on how the Torah is to be studied; how charity is to be given; the rules for commercial integrity; the Jewish home and family; the Sabbath and the festivals; the dietary laws; prayers and blessings. The final chapter considers the inner life of the Jew.

If it is not too presumptuous to say, the book is a kind of abridged *Shulḥan Arukh*, ("Arranged Table," the title of the most authoritative code of Jewish law). But this book is descriptive not prescriptive. Preaching has its place in the synagogue, but is out of place in a book of this nature. Some care has been taken to lay the table with rich, spiritual food skilfully prepared by the ancient and modern masters. It is left to the reader to decide whether and how much to eat.

"Belief becomes more firmly engrained when it is put to work in deed."

2

Study of the Torah

The Quest for Torah is Torah

It might seem odd, at first, to begin a book dealing with Jewish practice with a chapter on the study of the Torah. What has study to do with practical observance? First, it is impossible to keep the *mitzvot*, the practical observances of Judaism, without some knowledge of what they are and of how they are to be carried out. This knowledge can only be acquired through careful study. Secondly, and more significantly, the study of the Torah is itself a most important *mitzvah*. Even after the basic knowledge of how to perform the *mitzvot* has been acquired, the obligation to study the Torah is still as binding as ever. That is why scholars, long familiar with how to live as Jews, still spend as much of their time as they can studying the Torah. They hardly need to do this in order to learn how to keep the *mitzvot*. Study is not only a means to an end but an end in itself.

Study vs. Prayer

The Talmud tells of a rabbi who seemed to his colleague to be spending too much time saying his prayers when he could have spent it more profitably studying the Torah. The friend said to the praying rabbi, "You neglect eternal life [the study of the Torah] to engage in temporal existence [prayer, which includes petitions for worldly success]."

Prayer was supremely important for the Rabbis, but the study of the Torah was the most sublime aim of their lives.

A well-known talmudic passage says that in the second century of the present era, the Rabbis debated which is greater, study or practice. Eventually they took a vote on the issue, deciding that: "Study is greater because it leads to practice." At first glance this statement is puzzling. If the Rabbis say that study is important because it leads to practice, then they appear to suggest that study is the means, practice the end. How, then, can study be greater than practice? A person wants to get from London to New York. If the only way is to fly there, then the flight is indispensable; but the aim is not the flight. It is the destination that matters most.

The Rabbis' statement really means that the study of the Torah has a dual purpose: Study leads to practice and is itself practice. To carry out the *mitzvot* is a high privilege, but it involves practice alone; whereas in study there is both the *practice* of a *mitzvah* (of studying the Torah) and, in addition, the knowledge that leads to all other practices.

Maimonides: On Study

This is how Maimonides formulates the obligation to study the Torah:

"Every man in Israel has an obligation to study the Torah, whether he is rich or poor, whether healthy or a sufferer from ill-health, whether young or so old that his vigor has gone. Even if he is a poor man who has to beg at the door, and even if he has a wife and family to support, he is obliged to set aside some of his time by day and by night to study the Torah."

Maimonides, following rabbinic sources, speaks of the obligation of *men* to study the Torah. In this view women have no such obligation (except for that aspect of study required in order for them to know how to carry out the *mitzvot*), though Maimonides does say that if a woman studies the Torah she is rewarded for doing so. Nowadays, even in the most traditional circles, it is far from unusual for women to participate in Torah studies.

Much has been written on the way in which attitudes towards the role of women in Judaism have changed radically from those which prevailed in the Middle Ages. The point to be made in this connection is that the discussion about how changing attitudes affect Jewish observances is itself part of what is meant by study of the Torah. To study the Torah is not only a matter of getting to know the ancient texts. It is that, of course, but in addition it involves grappling with new problems and with social questions not envisaged in the old texts. There is ample room for debate, for questioning, for historical understanding. Study of the Torah, if it is to be real study, demands far more than the mental assimilation of facts. It involves a search for truth and the acknowledgment of uncertainty in matters about which certainty is not to be had or only to be had after rigorous searching. All this is part of the process. The quest for Torah is itself Torah.

Setting Up a Program of Study

Which program should be adopted for Torah studies? Based on traditional teachings it can be said that the best scheme is to have a study program that leads to knowing something about everything and everything about something. One should aim eventually to have a degree of familiarity with the whole range of Jewish learning—Bible, Talmud,

Maimonides wrote: "Every man in Israel has an obligation to study the Torah."

"Even after the basic knowledge of how to perform the mitzvot has been acquired, the obligation to study the Torah is still as binding as ever."

Jewish law, Jewish philosophy, theology and mysticism, Jewish history and literature—while studying one or another of these subjects in depth, leading to some expertise in that subject. This in-depth study should be chosen by personal fondness for the particular subject. One person will prefer the Bible, another will be attracted by the Talmud, yet another will find Jewish mysticism alluring, and so forth.

In studying, both range and depth are to be cultivated. A wide range of studies on its own can be extremely superficial, never penetrating to the profundities in every subject of Torah study. Study in-depth on its own can similarly be very one-sided. An expert, it has been suggested by educators, is a person who knows more and more about less and less. Care must be taken that the expert is not left knowing more and more about less and less until he ends up knowing everything about nothing.

A Single Page of Talmud

It used to be said of Rabbi Isaiah Karelitz that he was capable of studying a hundred pages of Talmud in a single day. His friends were doubtful about that, but this they did know: he sometimes spent a hundred days in the study of a single page.

Although there have been great Jewish scholars who were virtually self-taught and who studied all their lives on their own, the ideal is to begin to study at the feet of a competent teacher and then with a companion or as a member of a study group. The best way of grasping the subtleties of a subject (for most people the only way) is by discussing it with others, mind sharpening mind. The best method of all, once one has acquired sufficient knowledge and skill, is to learn by teaching others. Rabbi Judah the Prince, the editor of the Mishnah, once declared: "I have learned much from my teachers; more from my companions; and most of all from my disciples."

In devising a program of study, both range and depth are important.

The Ideal Student

In *Ethics of the Fathers* there is a list of forty-eight requirements for the ideal student. These are: mouthing the words of the text; pronouncing these distinctly; understanding the text and using discernment; studying in a spirit of awe, reverence, humility, and good cheer; ministering to the wise; having good fellow students; arguing with students; serenity of mind; having a knowledge of Scripture and Mishnah; engaging in moderation in business, in worldly matters, in pleasures, in sleep, in conversation, in laughter; having patience; being good-natured; having confidence in the wise; tolerating one's suffering; recognizing one's place; rejoicing in one's lot; caution in speech; claiming no credit for achievement; being a lovable person; loving God and all His creatures; loving righteousness; straight dealing and rebuke; keeping aloof from fame; having no pride in one's learning; having no personal pleasure in rendering decisions; bearing the yoke with one's companions and judging them favorably and helping them in their pursuit of truth and peace; being composed in study; asking questions and attempting to provide solutions; listening and then adding to the information imparted; studying in order to teach and to practice; making one's teacher wise; attending carefully to what he says; and repeating a teaching in the name of its author, giving the author the credit that is his due.

Hebrew and English

The Hebrew language is the key with which to unlock the gates of Jewish learning. It is desirable for the serious student to learn Hebrew, not at all a difficult proposition nowadays with so many courses in the language and with the possibility of study in Israel. However, a lack of knowledge of Hebrew should not be a cause for despair. Most of the classical works of Judaism are available in English translation, more or less faithful to the original. Many of the nuances will undoubtedly be lost even in the best translations, yet, after all, the main ideas in the texts can still be grasped.

Sources in Translation

For the Five Books of Moses there is the widely used *Pentateuch and Haftorahs* by Chief Rabbi Dr. J. H. Hertz (The Soncino Press, London, 1960). The "Hertz Chumash" contains a very readable commentary and notes from the Orthodox point of view. *The Torah*, edited by Rabbi W. Gunther Plaut (New York, 1981) provides a commentary and learned notes from the Reform point of view. (It is a fruitful exercise to note how the two commentaries differ and why.) For the Bible, as a whole, there is the new translation of the Jewish Publication Society of America (Philadelphia, 1982) and for a commentary on the whole of the Bible (except the Pentateuch) there is the series edited by Dr. A. Cohen, published by the Soncino Press (London, 1950).

The Soncino Press has also published an English translation, in thirty-five volumes, of the whole of the Babylonian Talmud, under the

Study is not only a means to an end but an end in itself.

"The best method of study is to learn by teaching others."

editorship of Rabbi Dr. I. Epstein (London, 1952). The Mishnah has been translated into English with an introduction and brief notes by the non-Jewish scholar, Herbert Danby (Oxford University Press, 1933) and by the Jewish scholar Philip Blackman in seven volumes with the Hebrew text and a useful supplement (London, 1956).

For the texts of medieval Jewish philosophy there are: Saadia Gaon's *Beliefs and Opinions*, translated by Samuel Rosenblatt (Yale University Press, 1948); Judah Halevi's *Kuzari*, translated by Hartwig Hirschfeld (London, 1951); Bahbya Ibn Pakudah's *Duties of the Heart*, translated by M. Hymanson (New York, 1945); Moses Maimonides' *Guide for the Perplexed*, translated by M. Friedländer (London, 1936) and, more recently, under the title *The Guide of the Perplexed*, translated by Shlomo Pines (Chicago University Press, 1953).

The *Zohar* has been translated into English by Harry Sperling and Maurice Simon, published in five volumes by the Soncino Press (London, 1959).

The above are only a very few of the works available in English. For further information regarding translations and many other aids to study, two extremely useful bibliographies should be consulted. These are: *The Study of Judaism: Bibliographical Studies* by various authors (Anti-Defamation League of B'nai B'rith, New York, 1972), and Judah Goldin and Seymour Cain's *A Reader's Guide to the Great Religions*, edited by Charles J. Adams (New York, 1971, pp. 283–344).

Two indispensable aids for Jewish studies are: *The Jewish Encyclopedia*, edited by Isidore Singer (Funk and Wagnalls, New York and London, 1926) and *Encyclopedia Judaica*, edited by Cecil Roth (Keter, Jerusalem, 1971). Three recommended one-volume Jewish histories are: *A History of the Jewish People*, by Max L. Margolis and Alexander Marx (Philadelphia, 1944); *Short History of the Jewish People*, by Cecil Roth (London, 1959); *A History of the Jews*, by Solomon Grayzel (Philadelphia, 1968).

How to Approach a Text

When studying a particular text, the student should first examine the historical background for which the information will be provided in the encyclopedias, the histories and, often, in the commentaries to the text. If, for example, the biblical Book of Amos is studied, one must first discover what was happening in the Northern and Southern Kingdoms at the time of the prophet; what prophecy meant in this period; what is denoted by the profession of herdsman (was Amos a simple peasant or was he a gentleman-farmer?); who the "sons of the prophets" were and what was their function; whether the words are those of Amos himself or were written down by his followers at some later date.

Since study is engaged in as a religious exercise (it is, after all, in pursuit of a *mitzvah*), the student will approach the text in a reverential spirit, seeking to discover in the book some message for contemporary Jewish life. But here lurks a danger. If the text is made to apply directly to the present situation, only distortion will result. It is possible to think of the prophet Amos, for example, as if he were alive today, speaking to us directly as if he had in mind our problems. At first, however, it is necessary to understand what it meant to bring God's words about justice and righteousness in the time when Amos lived—a time when social, political, and economic conditions were vastly different from those in our kind of society. In other words, the first task of the student of a classical Jewish text is to see it against the background of the time when it was composed. Only then does it become possible to discover how the inevitably time-bound text manages to convey truths for all time. Unless this is appreciated one will simply be reading into the text ideas that never were nor could have been in the mind of the ancient author.

"Since study is a religious exercise, the student will approach the text in a reverential spirit."

An Example of Scriptural Application

"When you see the ass of your enemy lying under its burden and would refrain from raising it, you must nevertheless raise it" (Exodus 23:5). Very few of us, nowadays, can ever apply this text to our lives. We do not have enemies with donkeys struggling under their burden. But implied in the text is that we should help even someone we do not like who is stranded by the roadside with a flat tire on his automobile, and that we should have compassion for animals in pain. Direct application is meaningless. Indirect application is highly significant.

Having attained a knowledge of the background and having projected himself or herself into that background, the student can proceed to the actual study of the texts. The particular words and sentences will be noted as well as how the whole of a passage is structured. A number of further questions will be asked. Is the text prose or poetry, or is it a mixture of both, and what difference does this

Students of Torah are not merely permitted to ask questions but are encouraged and even required to do so.

"Proper study involves at least as much asking the right questions as finding the right answers."

make? What is the relation of the text to other similar texts? How far is the author original, and how much has he been influenced by the ideas and the styles of others? Is the text a factual record of what its author thought, or have there been editorial revisions, and if there were, why did the editors see fit to revise the text? These and many other questions will usually be discussed by the standard commentaries and then the student will have to decide which answers are the most plausible.

The student will then raise further questions of his or her own. It can be maintained that there can be no real progress in study without questions being asked. Proper study involves at least as much asking the right questions as finding the right answers.

Questions?

The old story has it that a Jew was asked: "Why do Jews always answer a question with a question?" His reply: "Why not?"

The Reward for Study

Can one buy a share in the reward for studying the Torah? One can, according to the tradition, but only in certain circumstances. If *A* supports *B*, a scholar, so that *B* can study the Torah without financial worries, *A* has a share in *B*'s learning since it is *A* who has made the learning possible. But if *B* has already studied a good deal of the Torah and then *A* makes him an offer to buy a share in his learning, it is to no avail. The Torah is not a commodity to be bought and sold.

Never Ending

Study of the Torah is never ending. The Gerer Rebbe asked a young man, "Can you learn?" "A little," replied the young man. "That is all any of us can learn, only a little," said the Rebbe.

Helping Others to Study

Included in the *mitzvah* of Torah study is to help others to study by becoming, if one can afford it, a patron of learning. The traditional idea is that to provide material support for students and scholars to enable them to devote their time to learning is to enjoy some of the reward that is theirs. Even if one cannot afford to emulate the great Jewish patrons of learning it is still possible to make some contribution to institutions of Jewish learning. Especially those unable to study much themselves for one reason or another can have a share in Jewish learning by their support of scholars. The Midrash uses for this purpose the verse: "Rejoice, O Zebulun, on your journeys, And Issachar, in your tents" (Deuteronomy 33:18). Zebulun is the merchant traveling on his business with no time to spare for his studies. Issachar is the prototype of the scholar in the "tent" of learning, whom Zebulun supports so that he can study. Zebulun can rejoice while on his journeys because, although not a scholar himself, he has a share in the learning of Issachar.

3

Charity and Benevolence

Kindness and Righteousness

The two terms *tzedakah* and *gemilut ḥasadim* refer to generous actions and have long been key concepts in Jewish life. *Tzedakah* (literally "righteousness," doing the right thing, behaving in the right way) refers to financial assistance to the poor, while *gemilut ḥasadim* (literally "bestowing kindnesses," benevolence) is a broader concept embracing all good deeds on behalf of others.

The Talmud remarks that *tzedakah* only applies to the poor, whereas *gemilut ḥasadim* applies to the rich as well (a rich man frequently requires help of one kind or another). *Tzedakah* only applies to the living, whereas *gemilut ḥasadim* can be exercised on behalf of the dead as well. By attending a funeral an act of kindness is done on behalf of the deceased.

Tzedakah involves only the giving of money, whereas *gemilut ḥasadim* involves the giving of oneself in other ways: a kind word, a sympathetic ear, a helping hand, a friendly pat on the back, the sharing of a good story, a message of encouragement and hope, the giving of sound advice, lending books, giving someone a lift, inviting guests to the home.

All around us, we find opportunities to bestow kindness.

12

What is *gemilut ḥasadim*? A kind word, a sympathetic ear, a helping hand.

Tithing

In Temple times there was an elaborate system of tithing from agricultural products—corn, wine, oil, and fruit—for the benefit of the priests and Levites (who had no portion of their own in the land) and for the poor. The corners of the field were left unharvested for the poor to come in and gather for themselves. Sheaves of corn that were overlooked while gathering the harvest were left for the poor. In the Book of Ruth there is an idyllic picture of the benevolent farmer, Boaz, allowing Ruth and other poor people to gather the gleanings in his field.

In every Jewish community of talmudic times, there was a system of poor relief. Collections of food, drink, and money were made by voluntary overseers and distributed to the poor of each town. Poor people from other towns who were simply passing through had to be given lodging for the night and food each day of their stay.

All these rules applied to an agricultural community. Yet in many communities, even if they were not agricultural, the custom arose of tithing all income. This became known as *maaser kesafim*, "tithing

The smallest of coins in a *pushke* (charity box) represents the ancient Jewish principle of *tzedakah.*

The Mishnah: On the Poor

Many of the details regarding poor relief in ancient times are given in the Mishnah (*Peah* Chapter 8). There it is stated that the definition of a poor man allowed to apply for poor relief is one who has two-hundred zuz (a fairly large amount) in ready cash or fifty zuz invested in a commercial enterprise. If a rich man on a visit to a strange town has run out of money he may accept poor relief while in the town, but Rabbi Eliezer holds that when he returns home he should repay whatever he has taken. The Sages, however, hold that there is no need for him to repay since "at that time he was poor."

(*Peah* 5:4)

of money." Some authorities hold that to give a tenth of one's income each year in this way is more than a custom. It is a law, a real obligation. Others hold that there is no obligation to set aside such an amount each year, but it is a custom of the pious.

Whether law or custom, many devout Jews still follow the practice of setting aside a tenth of their annual earnings for charitable purposes. According to the Talmud, however, even an exceptionally generous person should not give away more than a fifth of his wealth because this might lead to his own impoverishment, and he may then himself be in need of assistance. It is unfair for someone, by his extreme generosity, to put an unduly heavy burden on the community. Nevertheless, in times of great distress and poverty the Jewish teachers have advised people who are relatively affluent to disregard this restriction.

The Shulḥan Arukh: On Charity

A section of the *Shulḥan Arukh,* the authoritative code of Jewish law compiled in the sixteenth century, says this on the subject of charity:

"How much should be given to a poor man? *Sufficient for his need in that which he wants* (Deuteronomy 15:8). This means that if he is hungry he should be fed; if he has no clothes he should be given clothes; if he has no furniture, it should be bought for him. Even if he was once accustomed, when he was rich, to ride a horse with a slave running in front, if he has now become poor a horse and a slave should be bought for him. [This should probably be understood as a temporary injunction, a way to let him down slowly.]

"So, too, each poor person should be given that which is appropriate for his needs. One who needs a morsel of bread should be given a morsel of bread; a whole loaf, he should be given a whole loaf; a bed, he should be given a bed. One who needs to be given bread hot from the oven, should be given bread hot from the oven. One who prefers bread that is cool, should be given bread that is cool. If the poor man is single and wishes to marry, he should be provided with the means to marry. A house should be rented for him, a bed and other furniture should be purchased for him, and then a wife found for him.

"But it would seem proper to hold" that all this only applies to the distribution of charity or to the community acting as a unit. An individual is not obliged to give the poor man 'sufficient for his need,' but the poor man should make his anguish known to the community. Where this is not possible the individual should give him what he needs if he can afford to do so."

(*Shulḥan Arukh, Yoreh Deah* 250:1)

How to Give

When helping the poor it is essential to avoid causing them any embarrassment. Maimonides goes so far as to say that it is better not to give alms at all than to give in a condescending, insulting manner. To humiliate another human being is unforgivable. Rabbinic hyperbole has it that one who brings another to public shame has no share in the World to Come. Tact and feeling should always be present in the donors of charity. That is why giving through charitable institutions is preferable (unless, of course, the poor require immediate assistance or they are too sensitive to apply to the institution). When giving is done in this way the benefactor is unaware of the identity of the recipients, and they are relieved of the need to show their gratitude.

"It is better not to give alms at all than to give in an insulting manner."

To Be Given the Best

Maimonides observes that where possible, the poor should be given of the best, not the leftovers from a rich man's table or the clothes he no longer can wear.

A Pretender

In the Jewish tradition a poor man, if he is really poor, not a pretender, has a right to be assisted. There is a Jewish tale of a beggar who regularly received a donation from a wealthy man. One day the man told him: "I am sorry I cannot give you anything. You see, my son has incurred heavy gambling debts and I have had to help him out." The beggar replied: "If your son wants to gamble let him gamble with his own money, not with mine!"

There is a priority of importance in the distribution of charity, based on ideas of fairness. The order of this precedence is: 1) a near relative who is poor (the closer the relationship the greater the priority—poor parents, for instance, must be assisted before poor uncles and aunts); 2) the poor of one's own town; 3) the poor of other towns. Naturally this precedence only refers to an individual donor who gives out of his own pocket. A charity administrator who has collected money from various people must never give more to his relatives simply because they are his relatives. The distribution, in this instance, must always be aboveboard, without the faintest suspicion of favoritism.

To be an officer of a charitable organization entails a heavy responsibility. It is all too easy to offend—perhaps unwittingly—both the donors by too much importuning and the poor by appearing too callous. The Talmud, aware of the problem, states that charity administrators sometimes deserve to be dubbed "oppressors" of the people, and yet their reward is greater than that of the donors.

The highest form of charity, say the Jewish teachers, is to help others with financial problems so that they are saved from becoming poor: for example, by putting some business in their way or by helping them to obtain gainful employment.

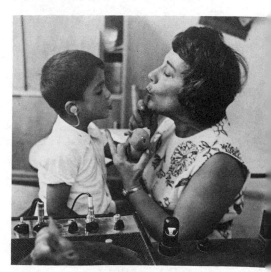

A deaf child learns to speak with the aid of a skilled teacher. To help a person become more independent is one of the higher forms of *tzedakah*.

**Ethics of the Fathers** on Charity:

"With regard to charity there are four different types of person. The person who wishes to give but does not want others to give [that is, he wants all the credit for himself] has a bad eye with regard to others [he cannot bear to see others doing good]. The one who wishes others to give but does not want to give himself, he has a bad eye so far as he himself is concerned [he likes the poor to be helped but does not see why he should contribute where there are richer people in the community]. One who gives and wishes others, too, to give is a saint [in the matter of charity]. One who neither gives himself nor wishes others to give is wicked [in the matter of charity]."

(_Ethics of the Fathers_ 5:13)

A Ḥasidic rebbe was seen giving a coin to a man with a bad reputation. "How can you give such a person charity?" his disciples asked. The rebbe replied: "I cannot be more particular than God who gave the coin to me, and look at my bad reputation."

To Give—and to Receive

> _"The highest form of charity is to prevent a person from becoming poor."_

The talmudic Rabbis advise that wherever possible a person should live frugally rather than rely on the assistance of others. The ideal is to earn one's own living, however hard that may be, and trusting in God to provide. Nevertheless, one who is in real need and yet refuses assistance is a sinner. The old Yiddish saying has it that if a poor person allowed himself to starve to death rather than apply for poor relief, such a person did not die of hunger but of pride.

Jewish traditional teaching urges that charity be given to Gentiles as well as to Jews and that benevolent acts be carried out on behalf of Gentiles as well as Jews. This principle is called "for the sake of peace," that is, promoting harmony in human society. The Rabbis who first taught this lived among idolaters whose conduct was far removed from the standards taught by the Torah. Yet the Rabbis still maintained that "for the sake of peace" there should be no discrimination in the matter of charity and benevolence. Nowadays, Jews are equally generous in contributing to non-Jewish and Jewish charities.

Gemilut Ḥasadim

Visiting the sick falls under the heading of _gemilut ḥasadim_. A sick person should be helped towards recovery not only by the physicians and nurses but by everyone able to help. Is it permitted to pray that an incurable person suffering great agony should die? The famous fourteenth-century teacher Nissim of Gerona so interpreted a talmudic passage that it positively advocates praying for such a person to die.

Others do not allow it for the sick person's immediate family who may have the unconscious motivation to be relieved of their own need to care. In these matters it must ultimately be left to the individual conscience.

Welcoming the Stranger

That our patriarch Abraham was a skilled practitioner of *gemilut ḥasadim* is especially evident in the generous hospitality he displayed towards travelers. The Bible relates (Genesis 18:1—2) that when Abraham saw three strangers approaching his tent during the hottest part of the day, he "ran to meet them," leaving the presence of God (who had at that same moment appeared before him). The Rabbis comment that welcoming wayfarers into your home is an even greater good than welcoming the presence of God.

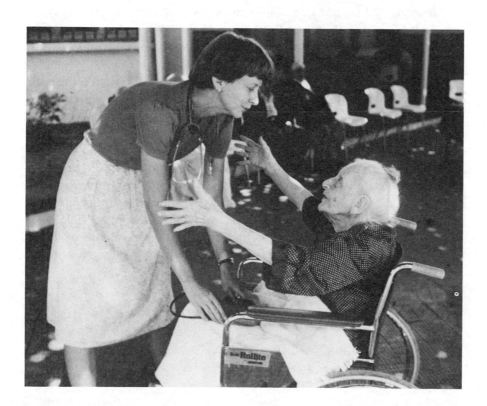

Doctors are practicing *gemilut ḥasadim* when they give kindness, as well as medical knowledge, to their patients.

How Not to Bring Comfort

Delicacy of feeling is required when visiting the sick. The visitors should not overstay their welcome or tell boring tales about their own illnesses. The traditional greeting when visiting the sick is *refuah shelemah*, "may you enjoy a speedy and complete recovery." There must not be the faintest hint to the sick that they have only themselves to blame for their illness, whether because they have sinned—as Job's friends suggested to Job—or for any other reason. Job's friends loved him, but evidently believed that they were called upon to de-

Comforting Those Who Mourn

Rabbi Israel Salanter, the founder of the Musar movement, was known as a man of very few words. Yet one day he was heard having a long discussion about a very mundane subject. When asked why, he replied that the man he was talking to had just suffered the loss of a close relative. The man's need for cheerful conversation was greater than Rabbi Salanter's desire for contemplative silence.

Another story is told about Rabbi Salanter's legendary capacity for kindness. At the end of his life he lay ill on his deathbed, alone except for a single attendant who suddenly became seized with fear. Although he himself was about to die, the rabbi spoke to the attendant with soothing words. Up to his very last moment he was trying to impart a note of warmth and comfort to others around him.

fend God, who brought the sufferings upon Job. So they suggested that Job deserved all he got because he was a secret sinner. Job was outraged by the suggestion, and the author of the book seems to have intended his readers to share Job's anger. God does not need to be defended by causing hurt and alarm to those in distress. The Rabbis explicitly say that it is a serious offense against Judaism's ethical standards to act as "Job's comforters." Such behavior is not the way to help those who suffer.

For the same reasons of tact and sensitivity, say the Rabbis, one who bears a grudge against a sick person should not visit that person, even if his motives are sound. The sick person may conclude that the visitor has come to gloat. Persons suffering from an embarrassing complaint should not be visited. Again it is virtually impossible to draw up hard and fast rules to be observed when visiting the sick. The general principle to be followed is that nothing should be said or done to make the sick person feel worse after the visit; everything should be said or done to make the sick person feel better.

4

Ethical Standards

"What the Lord Doth Require of Thee"

From its beginnings Judaism has had the strongest ethical orientation. Five of the Ten Commandments are purely ethical in content, and there is an ethical aspect to the other five. Judaism is sometimes described as "ethical monotheism." Like other generalizations about Judaism, this one is too neat and uncomplicated, but there is a good deal of truth in the idea that a Judaism with no high ethical standards set by God would be no Judaism at all.

If "religious" Jews declare that the important thing is to worship God without bothering too much about the welfare of their neighbors, they are not only deficient in ethics, they are not "religious" in any Jewish understanding of the term. Honesty, integrity, compassion, justice, righteousness—these values are stressed again and again as what God requires. The prophet Micah's wonderful prescription for the good life is too well known to require much further discussion: "It hath been told thee, O man, what is good and what the Lord doth require of thee; Only to do justly, and to love mercy, and to walk humbly with thy God" (Micah 6:8).

Unethical Business Practices

The biblical injunctions against cheating, theft, false weights and measures were extended by the Rabbis to include unethical conduct in general. Even though their society was very different from ours, it is not too difficult to see how the principles and concrete rules laid down by the ancient Rabbis can be applied today. For instance, the Rabbis give as an illustration of unfair trading that of the shopkeeper who polishes old utensils to make them look new and fetch a higher price; and of the butcher who uses certain devices to make his meat look fresher than it really is. They say further that one's "yes" should mean "yes" and one's "no" should mean "no," implying no subterfuge or reneging on one's word in business deals. In our society all this would militate against, for instance, cheating at examinations; claiming to have professional qualifications one does not have; giving or

" 'To do justly, to love mercy, and to walk humbly with thy God' (Micah 6:8)."

using false references for a position of trust; faking antiques; tampering with the car's odometer so the mileage appears less than it is; misleading advertising; employers taking unfair advantage of their employees, and employees failing to put in a full day's work. In our society there are usually laws against these kinds of practices, but it is notoriously easy to cheat without actually breaking the law. Judaism disapproves of unethical attempts to evade the law.

The thirteenth-century teacher Nahmanides notes that Scripture (Deuteronomy 13:19) speaks of "doing what is right in the sight of the Lord your God." "What is the significance of these words?" asks Nahmanides. Is it possible for a man never to go against the actual law and yet to be a thorough scoundrel? Such a man, Nahmanides says, may not be doing anything wrong so far as the law is concerned. If he is brought to court he will probably get off on a technicality. But God knows the truth. Judaism expects "doing what is right in the sight of the Lord your God."

Unethical Use of Words

It is utterly wrong to slander or libel others and to engage in any form of character assassination. There are two terms for this in the Jewish tradition: *lashon ha-ra* (literally, "evil tongue," talking evil about others, spreading malicious gossip) and *rekhilut* ("tale-bearing," telling *B* that *A* has spoken ill of him, stirring up mischief).

Just as it is wrong to speak *lashon ha-ra*, it is forbidden to listen to it. Poison pen letters would certainly fall under the categories of *lashon ha-ra* and *rekhilut*. There is another offense, which the Rabbis call *avak lashon ha-ra*. *Avak* means "dust." This offense involves speech that is quite harmless in itself yet which can result in harm to someone's reputation. It is not *lashon ha-ra* but the "dust" of *lashon ha-ra*. Examples of *avak lashon ha-ra* given by the Rabbis are: saying of someone that the fire for cooking is always burning in his home (implying that he is hospitable, but also, perhaps, that he and his family are gluttons); praising a man to his enemies (they may be moved to protest that he is not a good man at all and speak ill of him).

The Ḥafetz Ḥayyim

A Lithuanian talmudist, Israel Meir Kagan (1838–1933), noticing to his horror how rife malicious talk was in his poverty-stricken native land and how it had caused the disintegration of whole communities, resolved to compile a work listing all the rules and teachings on evil talk.

He called the work, which he published anonymously, Ḥafetz Ḥayyim, after the verses (Psalm 34:13–14) "Who is the man that desires life (he-ḥafetz ḥayyim), and loves days, that he may see good therein? Keep thy tongue from evil, And thy lips from speaking guile." To this day Rabbi Kagan is known in the Jewish world as the Ḥafetz Ḥayyim.

The Elixir of Life

Rabbi Alexandri once called out in the marketplace: "Who wants life, who wants life?" All the people gathered round him saying, "Give us life." He then quoted to them: *Who is the man that desires life, and loves days that he may see good? Keep thy tongue from evil.* (*Babylonian Talmud, Avodah Zarah* 19b)

There is sound psychology in the talmudic observation that if a man goes around constantly finding a particular fault in others, it is his own fault that he finds. Unconsciously aware of his inadequacy and lacking the courage to face it squarely, he compensates for his fault by finding fault in others, thereby feeling superior to them. The long life promised in the verse quoted above is to be understood not so much as a reward, but as a natural consequence of being at ease with oneself, avoiding strife, and refusing to make enemies. Persons who live like this are likely to enjoy a good and long life. The Ḥafetz Ḥayyim himself, though he published the work at the age of thirty-seven, lived until he was well into his nineties.

"The Talmud observes that the man who goes around constantly finding a particular fault in others is actually finding his own fault."

When to Speak Out

Are we then to understand that it is wrong to expose wickedness or to speak out against injustice? Not so, remarks the Ḥafetz Ḥayyim, quoting the possible translation of the verse (Leviticus 19:16): "Do not go around telling tales but do not stand by when your neighbor may be harmed." By all means do your utmost to avoid evil talk, but not when to fail to speak out will cause harm to the innocent. Two illustrations are given. *A* is about to go into business with *B*, someone he believes to be trustworthy. But you know that *B* is a crook. It is your duty to inform *A* that he is taking a risk. The second example: A girl has become engaged to a young man she believes to be healthy. But you know that, in fact, the young man has a disastrous medical history. It is your duty to inform her of the facts. She may love him enough to marry him even when she knows the truth, but then it will be her own free decision. The Ḥafetz Ḥayyim adds, however, that when telling the truth in such instances it must not be out of malice but solely because of the need to protect those who will otherwise suffer harm.

It follows from the above that Judaism would not approve of scandal and gossip sheets in which human failings, especially of the famous, are exposed to the curious as entertainment. But it would approve of investigative journalism where the motive is not merely for gain or to have a good story printed but primarily to uncover social abuses by those in power.

The Ḥafetz Ḥayyim

A critic by the name of Rosenfeld wrote scornfully of the *Ḥafetz Ḥayyim's* work, saying that if a Jew were to follow it he would never open his mouth. This was not the *Ḥafetz Ḥayyim's* intention at all. All who knew the *Ḥafetz Ḥayyim* testified that he was an excellent conversationalist, with a keen interest in a wide variety of topics and a colorful turn of phrase. He simply was a strong believer in the possibility of good talk without descending to *lashon ha-ra.*

Some rabbis, however, criticized his work on other grounds. They held that in this area a good deal depends on the particular circumstances and on the individual conscience, so that strict and definite rules and regulations as to when and when not to speak are out of place.

The Responsibility to Lead, not Mislead

"Do not place a stumbling block before the blind" (Leviticus 19:14). This passage literally refers to one who places in the path of a blind man an obstacle over which the blind man may fall and hurt himself. It is unlikely that even the most vicious person would ever be guilty of such a wrong.

The Rabbis, consequently, extend the verse to cover the encouragement of the morally and spiritually sightless and the misleading of the guileless who blindly place their trust in others. Examples given are: giving someone bad advice; selling weapons to criminals; helping others to do wrong; playing practical jokes; asking difficult questions of one unable to answer them in order to expose his ignorance. Dealing in drugs and encouraging drug-taking are obvious further examples. Some contemporary rabbis would include encouraging people to smoke cigarettes and some would even extend it to giving a smoker a light. Another contemporary example would be selling unsafe electrical appliances. It would certainly include the sale of contaminated food or the sale of nonkosher food as kosher.

Gambling

There is an opinion in the Talmud that all gambling is wrong because the loser only bets in his belief that he will win. When he loses he does not hand over the winnings with the degree of assent required for an agreement to pay to be binding. According to this view gambling is always an offense since the winner, by pocketing his winnings, is guilty of a form of theft, because he gains from a contract that is not legally binding. Most authorities reject this opinion, holding that the betting contract is legally binding like any other contract. Thus an occasional bet on a horse or a game of cards for money or buying a ticket in a lottery is not frowned upon. But an addiction to gambling is obviously to be avoided because, like any other addiction, it causes both psychological harm to the addict and distress to his family.

Although there are detailed discussions in the Talmud and Codes regarding the laws of damage to the person and property of others, there are many instances where there is no legal liability, but there is the strongest moral obligation not only to make good the damage but to take steps to assure that damage is not done in the first place. For instance, dogs and other animals that can do damage must be kept in strict control. Tanneries and other places that pollute the atmosphere must be kept at a distance from the residential areas of the town. Noise restrictions are also found in the talmudic sources. The great principle behind it all is that for the social contract to endure, each member of the society must play his or her part.

From the Talmud

Our Rabbis taught: The pious men of former generations used to hide their thorns and broken glass in the midst of their fields at a depth of three handbreadths below the surface so that the plough might not be hindered by them. Rabbi Sheshet used to throw them in the fire. Rava threw them into the River Tigris. Rabbi Judah said: One who wishes to be pious must be scrupulous in the observances regarding avoiding damage to others.

(*Babylonian Talmud, Bava Kama* 30a)

Our Rabbis taught: A man should not remove stones from his ground onto public ground. A certain man was removing stones from his ground onto public ground. A pious man saw him and said to him: "Stupid one! Why do you remove stones from ground that is not yours to ground that is yours?" The man laughed at him. After a time the man was obliged to sell his field and when he was walking on the public ground he fell over the stones he had put there. He then said: "How right was that pious man to say to me, 'Why do you remove stones from ground which is not yours to ground which is yours?'"

(*Babylonian Talmud, Bava Kama* 50b)

Avoiding Cruelty to Animals

To cause unnecessary pain to animals is a serious offense. Yet Judaism holds that animals may be used for human betterment. Medical experiments on animals for the purpose of increasing medical knowledge that will be of help to humans is allowed provided that care is taken to reduce the suffering of the animals to a minimum. Examples given in the sources are to pluck the feathers of a bird while still alive in order to obtain quills for pens, and for a coachman in a hurry to whip his struggling horse to achieve greater speed than it is normally capable of doing. It is not always easy to distinguish between the degree of pain to the animal that is allowed and the degree beyond this. In certain instances there is room for debate and reliance on the individual conscience.

There is no actual law against hunting animals for sport, but most Jewish teachers argue that it is contrary to the Jewish spirit of compassion to obtain pleasure from the pursuit of dumb creatures. It is not too easy to understand why Jews who would not hunt deer or birds for sport would still see no harm in fishing for sport. Perhaps it is because they imagine that fish do not feel as much pain as do animals and birds. On the other hand, very few teachers object to keeping animals in zoos or to Jews visiting zoos since the entertainment and information provided through the zoo outweighs the comparatively small amount of animal suffering caused by captivity. Trapping animals for their skins and furs and the use of these constitutes a similar gray area. To be taken into consideration is the excessive pain sometimes caused to the animals against the fact that there is human benefit; the livelihood of people engaged in the fur trade is also involved.

A number of Jews are vegetarians, but Judaism does not demand this. Indeed, it can be argued that to adopt vegetarianism on religious grounds—saying that it is morally wrong to kill animals for food—is to be more ethical and religious than the Torah wants us to be, implying a denial that Judaism is sufficient in moral values.

"While there is no explicit Jewish law against hunting for sport, it is nonetheless contrary to the Jewish spirit."

Keeping Pets

The Rabbis have no objection to the keeping of domestic animals in the house, although historically, it has never been an especially popular practice among Jews. This reluctance might have resulted from a desire to avoid the cruelty endemic to medieval Europe, when bears and roosters were often baited for popular amusement.

Today, of course, many Jews do keep pets. They are enjoined by Jewish ethical principles to take care of their pets lovingly, without excessive harshness and cruelty. There is even a rabbinic statement that one should feed dependent animals before feeding oneself, on the basis of a verse (Deuteronomy 11:15) in the Shema: "And I will give grass in the fields for thy cattle, and thou shalt eat and be satisfied." If God mentions the feeding of cattle before the feeding of people, the Rabbis reason, so then should people give food first to the animals entrusted to their care.

"Eat and Be Satisfied"

Rabbi Yitzhak Elḥanan Spektor of Kovno kept a pet cat, it is said, just so he could fulfill the biblical injunction of Deuteronomy 11:15. He never sat down to his own meal without first placing a saucer of milk in front of the cat.

Bal Tashhit

A passage in Deuteronomy (20:19) states that it is forbidden to destroy fruit-bearing trees. This commandment is known as *bal tashhit*, "do not destroy." The Rabbis extend the prohibition to any waste of natural resources.

From Maimonides' Code:

"It is not only forbidden to destroy fruit-bearing trees but whoever breaks vessels, tears clothes, demolishes a building, stops up a fountain or wastes food in a destructive way offends against the law of do not destroy.

(*Melakhim* 6:10)

The principle of *bal tashhit* is extended in the Jewish tradition to include squandering of one's wealth and talents (one of the objections to taking drugs is that they can damage the mind and destroy one's potential); harming the body with self-inflicted injuries (the medieval Rabbis never prescribed self-flagellation as penances for serious sins, unlike their Christian counterparts); and the preservation of nature's resources (the eighteenth-century Rabbi of Prague, Ezekiel Landau, ruled that while dangerous animals should be killed if they invade human habitation, it is wrong to hunt and kill them in their own haunts).

Where, however, the destruction is not a real waste at all but is to satisfy pressing human needs, it is permitted. It has never been suggested, for example, that Judaism objects to the lumber industry.

It is not too clear whether to spend lavishly on food when one can make do with less offends against the principle of *bal tashhit* (though it may offend on grounds of gluttony and ostentation). Believing that to be well-dressed is a virtue, the Rabbis advise a person to be comparatively frugal in spending money on food and drink, but to be liberal with the money spent on clothes. The Talmud tells of a Rabbi who, when passing through a field of thorns, would lift up his long robe to protect it even though this resulted in his legs being scratched. The scratches will heal, he remarked, but if the robe is torn it will be hard to repair. However, the Talmud also quotes a saying of the fourth-century teacher Rabbi Pappa, to the effect that one who prefers to drink wine when beer, a much cheaper drink, is available, offends against *bal tashhit*. But it must not be overlooked, as one of the commentators notes, that Rabbi Pappa was a manufacturer of beer!

Self-respect is encouraged in the Jewish tradition. Human dignity belongs to the whole human race; it is not given for an individual to demean himself since this would lower human dignity in general. Clowning, making a fool of oneself, should be avoided unless it is for the amusement of others or to make them feel at home. The body should be kept clean and wholesome.

Question:

A fruit-bearing tree, producing little fruit, has less value than the wood that will be obtained from it if it is cut down. May it be cut down or does this offend against the law of cutting down fruit-bearing trees?

Answer:

The Talmud (Bava Kama 91b–92a) states that if a fruit-bearing tree causes damage to other trees or if the value of its wood for fuel is greater than the value of the fruit it will produce, it is permitted to cut down the tree.

Tree-planting in a Jewish National Fund forest, Israel.

The Talmud tells of the great sage Hillel, who, as he went to the bathhouse, said to his disciples that he was going to carry out a religious duty. "What religious duty?" they asked. Hillel pointed to the statues of the emperor, which are washed regularly and kept in good repair. Humanity is created in God's image, he explained, and the human body must similarly be kept clean.

Some of the medieval Jewish thinkers state that human beings have three types of obligations: to God, to others, and to themselves. Self-realization may be a modern concept, but something very much like it is found in the earlier Jewish sources. Self-improvement is often stressed in the classical Jewish sources, though it is only right to point out that in these sources the meaning is that of progress to a spiritual goal, of coming closer to God.

On the basis of the verse, "You shall not make yourselves abominable" (Leviticus 20:25), the Rabbis say that it is wrong for a person to eat food that has become repulsive or to eat out of dirty dishes. Similarly, they include in this verse failing to perform natural body functions or witnessing sickening things.

As we have noted more than once, in this area of ethical conduct a good deal still depends on individual temperament and circumstances. When all the rules and principles have been stated, the individual conscience will yet have a voice. All that this chapter has tried to do is to sketch some of the ethical principles and a few of the ways in which these have been applied in the Jewish tradition.

Self-improvement is often stressed in classical Jewish sources.

5

Ritual Objects

Two Categories of Ritual Objects

Jewish religious objects are of two kinds: those that have a degree of sanctity and those that have no sanctity. There are sacred objects and religious objects. Belonging to the first category—sacred objects—are *mezuzah*, *tefillin*, and Sefer Torah. The objects associated with these attract some of their sanctity. These include the *mezuzah* case; the *tefillin* bag and, connected to the Sefer Torah, mantle bells, the *rimmonim* ("pomegranates," the ornaments fixed to the handles at the top), the crown, the pointer and the wrappings, and the curtain (*parokhet*) in front of the Ark.

These latter objects, however, only enjoy sanctity once they have been used, since their sanctity is imparted to them by the objects they serve. For example, once a curtain has been used as a *parokhet* in the synagogue it must not be used for any other purpose; but if it has not yet been used it may be used for other purposes. When these sacred objects are no longer suitable, when *tefillin*, for instance, have become unfit for use, they must not be casually discarded but must be buried (usually in the grave of a pious or learned Jew).

Belonging to the second category, religious objects that have no sanctity, are *tallit*, *tzitzit*, *shofar*, *sukkah* (but during the festival of Sukkot itself, the *sukkah* and its hangings must not be used for other purposes), *kiddush* cup, and Hanukkah menorah. These, as objects used for the performance of a *mitzvah*, should not be treated disrespectfully (for instance, they should not be thrown into the garbage), but they have no sanctity. They do not need to be buried when no longer fit for use, but may be burned. They can be used for other purposes, even while still fit for use as a *mitzvah*. It is permitted, for instance, to keep a wallet containing money in a *tallit* bag, but not in a *tefillin* bag.

The reason behind this distinction between sacred religious objects and nonsacred objects is that the former have the divine name inscribed on them. Each of these objects—the Sefer Torah, *tefillin*, and *mezuzot*—have been written especially by a scribe on parchment, for its own specific purpose, and as such are dedicated objects. The objects in the second category do not have this characteristic. The former are an end in themselves; the latter only a means to an end.

Synagogue

Into which category does a synagogue fall? It falls in between the two categories. During its use as a synagogue it must not be used for secular purposes: it is not permitted to eat and drink there, for instance. (There is no actual rule against smoking in a synagogue, but Rabbi David Hoffmann argued that since Christians would not dream of smoking in a church, Jews must never give the appearance of treating their religious buildings with less respect than their Christian friends treat theirs.) But when the synagogue is no longer in use it can be sold and used for other purposes. The assumption is that when a synagogue is consecrated it is done conditional on its use as such. The synagogue differs, then, from a Sefer Torah, *tefillin* and *mezuzot*, which are sacred in themselves. It is the use of the synagogue for prayer and worship that endows it with sanctity. When it is no longer used for these purposes, the synagogue loses it sanctity.

"The use of the synagogue for prayer and worship endows it with sanctity."

Mezuzah

In two Scriptural passages (Deuteronomy 6:4−6 and 11:13−21), it is stated that "these words" should be inscribed on the doorposts (*mezuzot*) of the house. The tradition understands this literally, to the effect that the two passages be inscribed on a strip of parchment and then fixed to the doorposts of the house. Although the original meaning of *mezuzah* is "doorpost," in the course of time the strip of parchment itself became known as a *mezuzah*. Since it is only fit for use when written by hand on parchment, a *mezuzah* should only be bought from reliable dealers. Unscrupulous dealers are guilty of tricking people into buying *mezuzot* that are printed or photocopied, and these are not on parchment but on ordinary paper.

The *mezuzah* contains, on one side, the two passages from Deuteronomy. These begin with the Shema: "Hear O Israel, the Lord our God, the Lord is One"—continuing with the rest of the first paragraph of the Shema and the second paragraph. On the reverse side it has become customary to write the letter *shin* at the top and three mysterious-looking words at the bottom. The *shin* stands for the divine name Shaddai, usually translated as "Almighty," though it is far from certain that this is a correct translation. The mysterious words represent the Hebrew words "the Lord our God the Lord"; but so as to avoid writing these as they are in the Torah and on the main portion of the *mezuzah*, they are written in code—each letter represented by the next letter to it in the alphabet (instead of *yod*, the letter *khaf*; instead of *hey*, the letter *vav*; and so on). The *mezuzah* is folded from left to right, and then either wrapped in paper or, more usually nowadays, placed in an attached *mezuzah* case. The *shin*, on the reverse side of the *mezuzah*, should ideally be visible—though this is not essential. Some *mezuzah* cases have an open space through which the *shin* can be seen.

"Since it is only fit for use when written by hand on parchment, a mezuzah *should only be bought from reliable dealers."*

"The Doors of Israel"

There is no doubt that the *shin* on the reverse side of the *mezuzah* stands for the divine name Shaddai. It is not only the *mezuzah* which has this name. The *tefillin* also have it, as we shall see, with the same meaning. Nevertheless, an interpretation of the *shin* has also been given which makes it especially appropriate to the *mezuzah*. According to this interpretation the *shin* does represent the word *shaddai*, but this is said to stand from **sh**omer **da**ltot **yi**srael, "guardian of the doors of Israel." The *mezuzah* stands guard at the doors of a Jewish home. This is best understood not as fire or burglary insurance but as spiritual protection. The home with *mezuzot* is a home in which God's word is always present to protect it from spiritual disintegration.

Attaching the Mezuzah

The *mezuzah* has to be fixed to the doorpost of each room in the house used for dwelling purposes, including the dining room, sitting room, bedroom, study, and any other room except small closets and, of course, the bathroom.

The place for the *mezuzah* is on the doorpost on the right as one enters the room. The authorities differ as to whether the *mezuzah* has to lie horizontally or vertically. To satisfy both requirements, it has long been the practice to place the *mezuzah* slanting upward. Since it is not upright it can be said to be more or less horizontal and since it does, after all, point upward it can also be said to be more or less vertical. In this ingenious way Jews have avoided the difference of opinion among the authorities, fixing the *mezuzah* so that it is correctly placed, in full accord with both opinions. The correct manner of fixing the *mezuzah* is, then, at the top third of the right-hand doorpost slanting upward towards the room as one enters. It is astonishing how many people have their *mezuzot* in the wrong position. If you place it as above you can score over your friends who have it in the wrong position or on the wrong doorpost (but whether one-upmanship in these matters is to be encouraged is another matter!)

The *mezuzah* can be fixed to the doorpost in any manner. It is usual to hammer it in with small nails, but recently *mezuzah* cases have been manufactured with glue on the back and this too is all right, provided that care is taken to see that the glue really holds. Before fixing the *mezuzah* this blessing is recited: "Who has sanctified us with His commandments and has commanded us to fix the *mezuzah*." Only one blessing should be recited no matter how many *mezuzot* are fixed to the rooms of the house. Some pious Jews, whenever they enter or leave a room, place the hand on the *mezuzah* and then put the hand to the lips.

A *mezuzah* from Eastern Europe. In the window is the Hebrew word *Shaddai*, a name for God.

Tefillin

In four Scriptural passages (Exodus 13:1−10; Exodus 13:11−16; Deuteronomy 6:4−6; Deuteronomy 11:13−21; these last two are the passages in the *mezuzah*, as above), there is a reference to the need for "these words" to be on the hand and between the eyes. According to the tradition, this too is taken literally: the four passages ("these words") are to be inscribed on parchment and placed in boxes; one box being bound by straps to the arm (the traditional understanding of the Hebrew *yad*, which can mean "arm" as well as "hand"), the other one to the forehead. "Between the eyes" is not taken to mean just above the nose but on the head itself "between the eyes," that is, not on one side but exactly in the middle. These parchment strips and the boxes in which they are contained are known as the *tefillin*.

The word *tefillin* seems to be the same word as *tefillah*, "prayer," and might mean objects worn during prayer. The difficulty with this derivation is that in talmudic times the *tefillin* were worn during the whole of the day, not only for prayer. Many scholars, consequently, see the resemblance of *tefillin* to *tefillah* as purely coincidental. They take the word *tefillin* either from *pillel*, "to judge" (the *tefillin* are the testimony to the unity of God), or from a root meaning "to attach," the *tefillin* being attachments to the head and the arm. Or it is also possible that in pre-talmudic times the *tefillin* were only worn during prayer.

There is evidence that in some communities in the Middle Ages there was a widespread neglect of *tefillin*. Faced with this neglect some teachers tried to justify it on the grounds that *tefillin* should only be worn by those completely clean in body and mind. The argument went that in times when a state of complete purity is difficult to attain, *tefillin* should be worn infrequently. Eventually, thanks to the efforts of the medieval preachers, who urged Jews to restore this important *mitzvah*, the wearing of *tefillin* became the norm for all devout Jews but no longer during the whole of the day, only for the morning prayers.

Young pioneers at a Youth Aliyah settlement in pre-war Palestine.

The Mezuzah and Superstition

Maimonides is very angry with the practice, in his day, of writing the names of angels and other incantations on the back of the *mezuzah*, or of writing the *mezuzah* so that it tapers to a point. All these practices, says Maimonides turn the *mezuzah* into a kind of amulet, instead of treating the *mezuzah* as a profound reminder of the unity of God. To have a *mezuzah* on the doorpost is to obey a divine commandment not to be used for magical purposes (of which Maimonides takes a dim view in any event). Presumably he would disapprove of the custom of wearing a *mezuzah* around the neck as a talisman or ornament. The same would apply to having a *mezuzah* on a car door. The way to prevent accidents to the car and its passengers is to drive carefully.

Wearing Tefillin All Day

Despite the fact that most Jews only wear *tefillin* during the morning prayers there have been especially pious folk who wore them all day. From Maimonides' description of the ideal sage who studied the Torah all day wearing his *tefillin* it looks as if Maimonides himself wore *tefillin* whenever he studied the Torah. The Vilna Gaon also wore *tefillin* all day. At one period of his life, Rabbi A. I. Kook had special *tefillin* made, which he could conceal beneath his hat and under his left sleeve so that he could wear the *tefillin* all day without a parade of excessive piety. Rabbi Isaiah Karelitz, the Ḥazon Ish, used to wear the hand *tefillin* all day similarly concealed beneath his sleeve so that others should not be aware of it.

The leather boxes into which the strips of parchment are placed are known as *batim*, "houses" (they "house" the *tefillin* sections). The *batim* have to be square and completely black. The straps of the *tefillin* must also be black. (It is not clear why they have to be black: perhaps to denote that because human capacity to apprehend God is extremely limited, there is an inevitable darkness.) The parchment of the *tefillin*, the boxes, and the straps must all come from a kosher animal. (One of the ideas here is that one does not use unworthy means to achieve a worthy end. The end does not justify the means.) All the four sections are written on a single strip of parchment for the hand *tefillin*. For the head *tefillin* there are four separate sections. Thus the hand *tefillin* box is in the form of a single cube while the head *tefillin* box is also a cube but one divided into four separate compartments, one for each of the strips of parchment. Like the *mezuzah*, the *tefillin* must be written by hand on parchment and should therefore only be purchased from a reliable dealer.

Each section of the head *tefillin* is wrapped around with a thin strip of the hair of a calf, and these hairs are made to obtrude through a tiny hole in the box. The reason given for this is that these hairs are a reminder of Israel's sin, when the people were faithless and worshiped the Golden Calf. Jews, the descendants of those idolaters, atone for their sin by wearing the *tefillin*, which emphasize God's unity.

Worked into the leather of the head *tefillin* box is a letter *shin*. The strap of the hand *tefillin* is made to produce a letter *yod*, and the strap of the head *tefillin* has a knot at the back shaped like the letter *dalet*. These three letters form the word Shaddai, the divine name, which we have noted in connection with the *mezuzah*. (Others have the knot of the head *tefillin* shaped like the letter *mem* so that the three letters form the word *shemi*, "My Name," i.e., the Name of God.)

There is an old tradition that the *shin* on the right-hand side of the head *tefillin* has three arms, while that on the left-hand side has four. The following is said to be the reason. In the rabbinic tradition there are 613 precepts in the Torah. Now the numerical value of the letter *shin* is 300. The two *shins* make a total of 600. Moreover, the word *shesh,* "six," is made up of two *shins,* giving us another six = 606. Add to this the three arms of the right side and the four on the left and we have another seven. Adding 600 plus 6 plus 7, we get a total of 613. The *tefillin* serve as a reminder of all the precepts of the Torah.

Rashi and Rabbenu Tam

In the Middle Ages there was a famous debate regarding *tefillin* between the famous French commentator, Rashi, and his equally famous grandson, Rabbenu Tam. (Actually it would seem that this difference of opinion preceded Rashi and Rabbenu Tam by several centuries.) The talmudic Rabbis insist that the sections of the *tefillin* must be written by the scribe in the order in which they appear in the Torah: Exodus 13:1–10; Exodus 13:11–16; Deuteronomy 6:4–6 (the Shema); and Deuteronomy 11:13–21. On this there is no dissenting voice. The debate centers around the question of how the sections are to be placed in the *batim*. Rashi (and Maimonides has the same opinion) holds that they have to be placed in the *batim* in the order in which they are written, the order in which they appear in the Torah. That is to say, for the hand *tefillin* they are written on the single strip of parchment in this order, and in the head *tefillin* they are placed in this order from the left of the wearer, which is the right of one facing the wearer. Rabbenu Tam holds, however, that they have to be placed with the Shema section (third in the order in which the sections appear in the Torah) at the end. Thus in the head *tefillin* the Shema section is placed on the outside, as if it were the fourth section. In the hand *tefillin* the Shema section is written third (since the writing has to be in the order in which the sections appear in the Torah), but a space is left between the second section and the Shema. The scribe can then write the fourth section in that space, making it appear to be the third section. (It is not too imaginative to see here the stress on correct ordering of things.)

The *Shulḥan Arukh's* ruling follows Rashi. However, some pious Jews, and all Ḥasidim, in order to satisfy both requirements, wear two sets of *tefillin,* those of Rashi and those of Rabbenu Tam. Some oriental Jews wear both sets of *tefillin* at the same time, but the more usual practice is to wear the Rashi *tefillin* for the first and main part of the morning service and then to switch to Rabbenu Tam's *tefillin* for the rest of the service. The *Shulḥan Arukh* rules that to wear both pairs of *tefillin* is a kind of showing off; it should only be practiced by one renowned for great piety. The actual ruling follows Rashi. The argument of the Ḥasidim and the others who wear the two pairs is that since so many do wear them it is no longer a parade of excessive piety to do so.

A man came to a synagogue one morning and wished to borrow a pair of *tefillin.* "You can't have those," said the shamash, "they are Rabbenu Tam's *te*fillin." "Don't worry," replied the man, "I daven very quickly and he can have them as soon as he gets here."

The Way to Put on Tefillin

This is the way to put on the *tefillin.* The hand *tefillin* is placed on the upper part of the left arm, on the muscle, and the first benediction is recited: "Blessed art Thou, who has commanded us to put on *tefillin."* The knot is then tightened, and the strap wound seven times around the arm. The head *tefillin* is then put on, and the second benediction is recited: "Blessed art Thou, who has commanded us concerning the *mitzvah* of *tefillin."* (Since some authorities do not have this second benediction, it is customary to recite after it the words: "Blessed be His glorious Kingdom for ever and ever," as if to say: "If I have recited an unnecessary benediction, and have therefore taken God's name in vain, I make up for this by blessing His Kingship.") The bottom end of the head *tefillin* should be on the hair of the head (or the place of the hair in the case of a bald man). No part of the head *tefillin* should be on the bare forehead. As we have noted, "between the eyes" means in the middle of the head itself. The strap of the hand *tefillin* is then wound once around the top joint of the middle finger and twice around the second joint of this finger. It is then wound in a slanting direction from between the little finger and the second finger towards the thumb, then between the thumb and the other fingers, then around the hand in a straight direction. When this is done there is another *shin* on the strap on the hand.

A left-handed man wears the hand *tefillin* on his right hand. It is the weaker hand that has the *tefillin,* perhaps to suggest that it is the weaker side of human nature that requires to be fortified by reflection of God and His purpose. The stronger side can take care of itself.

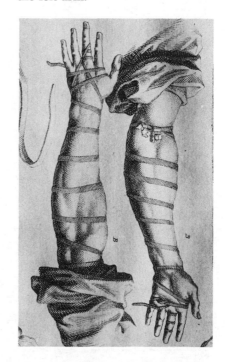

An eighteenth century drawing by Bernard Picart, illustrating the way the *tefillin* is wrapped around the left arm.

Symbolism of the Tefillin

The head *tefillin* is more sacred than the hand, since it contains four separate sections, whereas the hand *tefillin* contains only one strip of parchment. That is why the hand *tefillin* has to be put on first. One must always go higher in the pursuit of holiness.

The *tefillin* of the hand is more or less opposite the heart. The *tefillin* thus embrace head, heart, and hand, all three of which are to be used in God's service. The rule is that the hand *tefillin*, opposite the heart, must be covered by the sleeve to denote that one should not wear one's heart upon one's sleeve and not boast of the good deeds per-formed by the hand. One's good deeds and one's intimate relationship with God are not to be revealed to others. But the Jewish mind, represented by the head *tefillin*, should help to uncover the truth of the Torah and spread it abroad. The Jewish mind should be open and out-ward looking.

There are four compartments in the head *tefillin*, only one in the hand *tefillin*. Opinions differ and it is pointless to have agreement among all Jews on all matters. Yet the essential Jewish path is ideally uniform, all Jews worshiping God in the same way, the way recog-nized by the tradition of their ancestors.

God Wears Tefillin

In the Babylonian Talmud (Berakhot 6a–b), the Rabbis say that God Himself wears *tefillin*. What is written in the di-vine *tefillin*? The four sections of these *tefillin* have the words: "And who is like Thy people Israel, a nation one on the earth" (I Chronicles 17:21); "For what great nation is there ..." (Deuteronomy 4:7–8); "Happy art thou, O Israel" (Deuteronomy 33:29); and "To make thee high above all nations" (Deuteronomy 26:19). This is a quaint way of saying that if the peo-ple of Israel, by wearing *tefillin*, acclaim God's unity and their faithfulness to Him, He responds by keeping them always in mind.

Tzitzit

"It is the weaker hand that has the tefillin, *perhaps to suggest that it is the weaker side of human nature that needs to be fortified by reflection of God and His purpose."*

The *tallit* is often said to be a prayer shawl, but this requires some elaboration. Originally, the word *tallit* meant simply a robe or cloak and had no religious significance. But during the Middle Ages *tallit* became a religious object.

In the Book of Numbers 15:37–41 (paralleled by Deuteronomy 22:12), there is the commandment to attach *tzitzit*, "fringes," to the corners of the garment, the purpose being to remember the command-ments of the Lord. (Rather like, it has been suggested, our custom of tying a knot in a handkerchief to remind us of something.) In ancient times people regularly wore four-cornered garments, to which they at-tached the *tzitzit*. But only four-cornered garments require *tzitzit*, so in Western lands, where four-cornered garments were not generally worn, there was no need to have *tzitzit*, and the *mitzvah* was in dan-ger of being forgotten. Out of their love for the *mitzvot*, some of the medieval teachers came up with the suggestion that special four-cornered garments be woven and worn with *tzitzit* attached. This special garment is the *tallit* and since, eventually, it became the norm to wear the *tallit* during the morning service, when the text in Numbers is uttered as part of the Shema, the *tallit* did become a prayer shawl and so it has remained.

Many pious Jews also wear, underneath their outer clothes, a special small *tallit* with *tzitzit*, called *tallit katan* or *arba kanfot* ("four corners"). This garment enables one to extend the wearing of *tzitzit* to all times, not just during prayer. Since *tzitzit* have no sanctity, the *tallit katan* does not have to be removed when going to the toilet.

An Ingenious Interpretation

Rabbi Meir Simḥah Kagan of Dvinsk (1843–1926) gave an ingenious interpretation of the *mitzvah* of *tzitzit*. Without fringes, he said, a garment would be unattractive and incomplete. God did not create a finished world but left much for human beings to do to make the world a better place. God has woven the garment of the world, but we have to fix the *tzitzit*.

This idea is also found in the talmudic account in which the Roman governor, Turnus Rufus, asks Rabbi Akiba: "If God wants men to be circumcised why did He create them with a foreskin?" Rabbi Akiba suggests that God wants His creatures to perfect themselves. He wants the cooperation of humans in the fulfillment of His plans for them.

A Question of Intention

The *tzitzit* have to be woven for the express purpose of the *mitzvah*. The weaver has to have the intention of manufacturing fringes to be used as *tzitzit*. When machines were introduced to do the weaving in the last century, some rabbis objected to machine-woven *tzitzit* on the grounds that a machine cannot have the required intention. But the view prevailed that the intention of the person who works the machine is sufficient for the purpose.

How to Attach the Tzitzit to the Tallit

This is how the *tzitzit* are fixed in the *tallit*. (It is useful to know this so that if the *tzitzit* in a *tallit* become unfit for use, new *tzitzit* can be bought and attached to the *tallit* in the proper way.) A bundle of *tzitzit* will be found to consist of four long threads and twelve shorter threads. Take one long thread and three of the shorter threads and thread these through the hole in the corner of the *tallit*. You will now have four half threads on one side of the hole and another four on the other side (formed from the doubling of the threads downward). Tie a loose knot (to be undone after the fixing of the *tzitzit*) in the four shorter threads, so as to keep them together on the same side. Take four threads in one hand and four in the other and tie them together in a double knot. Then take the long thread and wind it seven times around the other seven. Tie another double knot, and then wind the long thread eight times around the other seven threads and tie another double knot. Take the long thread (shorter by now, but still longer than the others) and wind it eleven times around the other seven and tie a double knot. Finally, take the long thread again and wind it thirteen times around the other seven threads and tie another double knot.

You will now have a series of double knots and windings and eight threads hanging down, four on each side. The loose knot in the four that you made at the beginning should now be untied. Ideally all the windings should be of the same length. This is achieved by making the later windings a little tighter than the first two. At this stage the ends of all eight threads should be equal since by now the long thread should be as short as the others. Now repeat the process at the other three corners and you have a *tallit* fit for use.

There are four windings of the longer thread around the others: seven, eight, eleven, and thirteen, making a total of thirty-nine. "The Lord is One" (in Hebrew, the Tetragrammaton, which has the numerical value of twenty-six) and the word *eḥad* (one, which has the numerical value of thirteen), make the same total of thirty-nine. This is the usual explanation for this particular series of windings.

The Book of Numbers speaks of a blue thread in the *tzitzit*. According to the Talmud this blue dye was obtained from a marine animal known as the *ḥillazon*, the exact identity of which has long been unknown so that the blue thread is no longer used. The Ḥasidic rabbi, Gershon Henoch of Radzyn, in the last century, spent some time in the aquarium in Naples where he claimed to have found the *ḥillazon*. He set up a small factory for the manufacture of the blue thread, but was unable to persuade his colleagues to adopt the innovation. To this day Radzyner Ḥasidim (and the Bratzlaver Ḥasidim) still have the blue thread in their *tzitzit*. As a reminder of the blue thread, the manufacturers of the *tallit* around the early eighteenth century produced it with blue or black lines near the edge, and most have this today.

When to Put On Tallit and Tefillin

Ideally the *tallit* should cover most of the body. Some pious Jews wear the *tallit* over the head during the more important prayers. Others only see this as fitting for scholars. The purpose of covering the head with the *tallit* is to shut oneself off from the world and its distractions. Wrapped completely in the *tallit* one is alone with God. It is easy to see how this can be no more than religious ostentation.

A Tallit over his Head

In Orthodox communities in Germany, only rabbis and scholars were allowed to cover their heads with the *tallit.* A shamash once observed a man without scholarly attainments wearing his *tallit* over his head. The shamash said to him:

"Sir, since you wear your *tallit* over your head you must be a scholar. But if you are a scholar you must be aware of the rule that an ignoramus should not wear his *tallit* over his head!"

Tefillin are called a "sign" of God's presence. Consequently, they are not worn on the Sabbath and the festivals since then there are these other "signs," and the wearing of *tefillin* is unnecessary. The *tallit*, on the other hand, is worn on all days. On the basis of the principle that the more regular has precedence over the less regular, the *tallit* is put on before the *tefillin*. The *tallit* is more regular because it is worn on Sabbaths and festivals as well as the weekdays.

Boro Park, Brooklyn, 1981.

Women and the Mitzvot

If a house is occupied by a woman, or a number of women, and no men reside there, does it have to have *mezuzot*? Are women obliged to wear *tefillin* and the *tallit*? According to the traditional scheme, women have no obligation to keep those positive *mitzvot* which depend for their performance on a given time. The *mezuzah* does not depend on time (it is an obligation all the time) and so it is as binding upon women as upon men. *Tzitzit* and *tefillin* are not worn at night. Consequently these two *mitzvot* do depend on time, and women are not obliged to carry them out.

Various suggestions have been put forward for why women should not be obliged to carry out those *mitzvot* which depend for their performance on a given time. One suggestion is that married women have an obligation to look after their home and family and it would be unreasonable to expect them to be tied down, carrying out *mitzvot* that can only be performed at a given time. A mystical reason advanced is that the soul of women derives from a higher world, a world that is beyond time, so that time-bound *mitzvot* are not for them. Some modern observers see the exclusion of women from these *mitzvot* as a hangover from the institution of women priests in ancient idolatrous worship. In its struggle against any association with idolatry, the Torah excludes women from certain cultic rituals generally performed by the priests. The most gallant interpretation is found in a late Midrash. Here it is said that women are more religious by nature than men and less prone to sin. They do not require as many reminders of the good life as do men.

Although it follows that women have no obligation to hear the sounding of the *shofar* on Rosh Hashanah or to take the *lulav* and sit in the *sukkah* on Sukkot, there is no objection to women carrying out these *mitzvot* if they wish to do so. In fact, it has long been the practice in the majority of communities for women to carry out these *mitzvot* as an extra obligation they have taken upon themselves. Logic would demand that the same should apply to *tzitzit* and *tefillin*, but to date, it is unusual for women to carry out these *mitzvot*.

6 Marriage

Permitted and Forbidden Degrees

The forbidden degrees of marriage are listed in the book of Leviticus (chapters 18 and 20). There are also a number of secondary degrees (*sheniyot*) forbidden by rabbinic law. The forbidden degrees are too well-known to require further statement, but it should be noted that while an aunt may not marry her nephew, an uncle may marry his niece. The marriage of first cousins is also permitted. However, recent rabbinic voices have been raised to discourage the marriage of near relatives to one another, since advances in medicine have shown that in such unions there is greater risk of inherited disease to the offspring.

Step-brother may marry step-sister provided that they have no parent in common. For instance, a man *A* marries a woman *B* and they have a son *C*. *A* dies and then *B* marries *D* and they have a son *E*. *B* dies and then *D* marries *F* and they have a daughter *G*. *G* may not marry *E* because they have the same father, *D*. But *G* may marry *C* because there is no blood relationship at all.

Like all aspects of Jewish life, marriage has its legal aspects, with clear definitions of what is forbidden and what is permitted.

Polygamy

In biblical and rabbinic times polygamy was permitted; a man could have more than one wife. There is some evidence that even in ancient times monogamy was the norm. In the Bible, Adam has only one wife; and the prophets describe the relationship between God and Israel in terms of loyalty between husband and wife (not wives). Nearly all the Rabbis whose names are found in the Talmud had only one wife at a time. Nevertheless, polygamy was permitted until the so-called "Ban of Rabbenu Gershom" of around the year 1000, which forbade the practice (but applied only to Ashkenazim). Nowadays, with very few exceptions, monogamy is the norm for all Jews.

The Marriage Ceremony

The marriage ceremony takes place under the *ḥuppah* ("canopy"), a symbolic representation of the bridal chamber. Originally there were two separate ceremonies. The first, the formal marriage known as *kiddushin*, or *erusin* ("betrothal"), took place in the bride's house. She remained there for about another year, after which the actual marriage, *nisuin*, took place. In the second ceremony, bride and groom entered the *ḥuppah*, which in those days was not a canopy but the actual bridal chamber.

In the Middle Ages, probably in order to have proper communal control of Jewish marriages, the two ceremonies were combined. That is why there are two sets of benedictions in the present marriage ceremony: one set before the delivery of the ring—the *kiddushin*; and another set afterwards—the *ḥuppah*, or *nisuin*. Each set of benedictions is recited over a cup of wine from which the bride and groom sip. (It is the usual custom in Western lands for the wine to be handed to the couple by their parents, who stand beside them at the *ḥuppah*.)

The actual marriage is effected by the groom giving the ring to his bride and declaring: "Behold thou art sanctified unto me by this ring according to the law of Moses and Israel." (In Reform congregations it is usual for the bride to give her ring to the groom while making the same declaration.)

"Behold thou art sanctified unto me by this ring according to the law of Moses and Israel." Two perspectives of a wedding ring from early nineteenth-century Italy, with the Hebrew inscription *mazal tov*.

Ketubah

The *ketubah*, the marriage settlement providing for the maintenance of the wife and guaranteeing her a share of the husband's estate in the event of divorce or his death, is drawn up and signed during the ceremony. In communities outside the State of Israel, Jews follow the law of the land in financial matters such as these. For them the *ketubah* is a formality, though an important one. Instead of an amount determined by the husband's financial means, the *ketubah* will declare a fixed amount, generally two hundred zuz. (In ancient times two hundred zuz was a considerable sum. As we have noted earlier a person owning this amount could no longer qualify for poor relief.) It is now often the practice to have an artist draw the *ketubah*. The ancient, handwritten *ketubot* have become collector's items.

Where to Hold the Ceremony

There is no need for the ceremony to take place in a synagogue. In Hungary, Orthodox rabbis even declared a synagogue ceremony forbidden on the grounds that this too closely resembles a church wedding. The older custom, still followed in many communities, is to have the ḥuppah in the open air, symbolic of the heavenly protection the couple pray will be theirs.

Yet there is a good deal to be said for having weddings celebrated in the synagogue. When this is done the ceremony is more clearly seen for what it is, a profound religious act and affirmation. Since Judaism does permit divorce when a marriage has broken down, there are no vows by the couple to remain together until death, as in a church wedding. Obviously, however, it is implied that the union is for life and that nothing will be allowed to interfere with the couple's loyalty to one another.

Many of the wedding customs in Western lands are not Jewish at all, but have been adopted by Jews simply because that is the way weddings are celebrated where they live. There is no harm in this provided that the customs are not those of another religion. It follows that the frequent question—can a non-Jewish friend be the best man or a bridesmaid?—is to be answered in the affirmative. The best man and the bridesmaid are not Jewish institutions at all, and there is no reason why these functions may not be carried out by non-Jewish friends.

"It is now often the practice to have an artist draw a ketubah. *The ancient, handwritten* ketubot *have become collectors' items."*

Why Is a Glass Broken at the End of the Ceremony?

The breaking of the glass by the bridegroom at the end of the marriage ceremony has received many different interpretations. The widespread understanding of this custom as a symbol of the loss of virginity is quite unfounded, since a glass is also broken when the bride has been previously married. A number of scholars have traced the custom back to medieval Germany, where peasants would break things at a wedding so as to avert the jealousy of the demons. (The demons would then conclude that all was not well and decide to leave the couple alone.)

Whatever the origin of the custom, it has since been given a Jewish interpretation—that its purpose is to remind the couple of the destruction of the Temple. Even on such a happy occasion, bride and groom are to be aware of the calamities that have befallen their people. By building a truly Jewish home, based on the constructive ideals of Judaism, they will combat all destructive forces. A modern, romantic interpretation has also been given. Bride and groom declare that their love for one another will endure until the shattered glass becomes whole once again—a very long time.

The Mikveh

According to the Orthodox tradition, marital relations are to be avoided not only during menstruation but for seven days afterwards, and then they are to be resumed only after the wife's immersion in a specially constructed ritual bath, the *mikveh* (the word means "gathering,"as in a gathering of water). The full details of these laws are found in various booklets prepared for the purpose, though it must be admitted many of these are crude in their approach. The use of the word "unclean" for the *niddah* (menstruating woman) is unfortunate. It is not a physical uncleanness that is intended.

The cleansing provided by the *mikveh* is ritualistic and spiritual. An analogy can be found in the ritual washing of the hands before meals. The hands are not washed because of actual dirt. It is the ritual act of washing the hands from a vessel and the benediction recited over this that makes the act a form of religious preparation. Similarly, the whole idea of *mikveh* is to endow the marital act with religious significance. Each month the marriage relationship is renewed afresh with a religious act of high significance. It has been interpreted as a form of new creation, much as a convert to Judaism is first immersed in a *mikveh* to begin a new life as a Jew.

Details concerning the construction of a *mikveh* can safely be left to the experts, but basically the *mikveh* consists of a cistern into which is gathered rain water (that is, water untouched by human hands, considered to be pure water from Heaven). Connected to this

Tradition provides a ritual for spiritual purification, using God's pure water as its basic symbol.

cistern by a small aperture, which can be opened and shut when required, is a bath filled with ordinary tap water. The principle is that when the ordinary bath water touches the special water in the cistern, the bath water itself becomes spiritually pure. The bath water is, of course, heated and disinfected.

While it can no longer be said that many Jewish women use the *mikveh*, those who still do have testified to the process as a profound religious experience.

The Last Word

Who should have the last word where husband and wife differ? According to some of the ancient teachers, the husband should have the last word in a dispute about religious matters, but the wife should have it when in a dispute about secular or worldly matters. It was said, ironically, of a famous Rabbi, who made this arrangement when he married, that his wife had the worst of the bargain since for him everything was a religious matter!

Man and Woman, *Ish* and *Ishah*

A mystical tradition holds that the sexual act unifies the male and female aspects of God, thus creating harmony in the celestial spheres. The Hebrew words *ish* (man) and *ishah* (woman) are cited. They come together to form the union of the letters *yud* and *hay,* the first two letters of God's sacred name.

The sages of the Talmud considered dancing before the bride and groom to be a *mitzvah* in itself.

From the Talmud

A man should love his wife as much as he loves himself, but respect her more.
(Yevamot 63a)

If your wife is little you should bend down and listen to her.
(Bava Metzia 59a)

The Ark in the desert was tiny but the people could meet God there. Later, even the huge temple was not big enough. So people say about love, "When our love was strong we could sit on the edge of a sword. Now that our love is faded even the widest couch is too small."
(Sanhedrin 72)

The Standards in Jewish Marriage

The highest standards of conduct are demanded in a Jewish marriage. Husband and wife are expected to be completely faithful to one another throughout their marriage. During marital relations they must not have any other partner in mind and must have respect and consideration for one another. The husband especially is enjoined to be considerate to his wife, wooing her with tenderness and loving words.

Although in marital disputes there are faults on both sides, Jewish teaching generally makes the husband, in particular, responsible for promoting *shalom bayit*, "peace in the home." He should be the last to start a quarrel and the first to make it up. The Talmud states that a husband should avoid wounding words, an unfeeling attitude, and anything that brings tears to his wife. For a husband to resort to physical violence against his wife was entirely unthinkable to the Jewish teachers. To make peace between husband and wife is considered to be a great *mitzvah*.

"To make peace between husband and wife is considered to be a great mitzvah."

7

Birth and Education

Procreation

Children have always been considered a great blessing in the Jewish tradition. It is a religious obligation to have children. Naturally, the actual gift of children is from God, but the meaning of this *mitzvah* is that marriage is for procreation as well as for companionship. This idea is based on the verse: "God blessed Noah and his sons, and said to them: 'Be fertile and increase, and fill the earth'" (Genesis 9:1). There are a number of prayers in which the hope is expressed of having "children and grandchildren occupied in the Torah." A contemporary rabbi remarked that plants do not have offspring (the new plant only arrives after the decay of the old). Animals do have offspring, but they are never aware of the offspring of their offspring. Humans are alone endowed with the gift of "children and grandchildren."

According to the School of Shammai, this *mitzvah* is fulfilled when there are at least two male children, but the School of Hillel ruled (and this was followed) that the *mitzvah* is fulfilled when there are two children, one male and one female. It is because of this *mitzvah* that Judaism does not advocate celibacy even for those totally dedicated to the religion, unlike some other religions, which require their priests to be unmarried.

This fertility amulet from Tunisia reflects the very first commandment in the Torah: "Be fertile and increase, and till the earth." (Genesis 1:28)

47

Naming the Baby

A boy is given his Hebrew name at the *Brit.* A girl is named in the synagogue when the father is called up to the reading of the Torah (usually, but not necessarily, on the Sabbath after the birth). Among Ashkenazim, a child is not usually named after a living person. In addition to the name of a deceased relative, names are often chosen from those of biblical heroes and heroines (when, for instance, these names occur in the portion of the Torah or Haftarah read that week) or after famous Jews. Sometimes a name is given to mark an important event of the time. For example, there are women called Balfoura, who were born in the year of the Balfour Declaration.

Among Sephardim the name Mashiaḥ is found. It is suggested that this name was originally given when people thought the false messiah, Shabbetai Zevi, was the true messiah, and the name was then handed down through generations.

Where a boy is named after a woman, or a girl after a man, the name is slightly changed. If the grandmother was called Frieda (meaning "peace"), the boy can be called Efraim (which sounds like Frieda) or Shalom. If the grandfather is called Shlomo, the girl can be called Shulamit.

It is incorrect to choose the name of a biblical villain. Jews do not use the names Esau, Nimrod, Pharaoh, or Jezebel. The fact that a number of rabbis were called Ishmael is explained by the tradition that the biblical Ishmael repented of his misdeeds before he died and is, therefore, a biblical hero after whom it is good to name a child.

> *"Children are a great blessing in Jewish life. The gift of children is from God."*

After the Rebbe

Ḥasidim often called their sons after the rebbe who was the first leader of their group. Men named Sheneur Zalman belong to the Lubavitch movement (the Ḥabad trend in Ḥasidism); they are named after Rabbi Sheneur Zalman of Liady, the movement's founder. Many Gerer Ḥasidim are called Yitzhak Meir, after Rabbi Yitzhak Meir (the *Rim, Rabbi Yitzhak Meir*), who founded the Gerer dynasty in the nineteenth century.

The Brit

Since the *Brit* is always carried out by a competent *mohel* there is no need to describe the procedure in detail. The *mohel* will come beforehand to check the baby's health; he will then make all the arrangements. It is not essential for a *minyan* (the quorum of ten required for some other rituals) to be present at the *Brit*. The ceremony is usually followed by a celebration. There is an old tradition that if one is invited to a *Brit* one should not refuse, unless it is urgent to be elsewhere at the time. The *Brit* takes place on the eighth day after the birth and should not be postponed except for health reasons. Where the *Brit* does take place on the eighth day, it can and should be carried out even if that day is a Sabbath. The prayer for the baby at his *Brit* is: "As he has entered into the covenant [*brit* means "covenant"] so may he be spared to enter into [a life of] Torah, Ḥuppah, and good deeds." This order is interesting. Torah, of course, comes first, but good deeds, it is implied, can only come after marriage.

"Humans alone are endowed with the gift of both children and grandchildren."

According to tradition, those in attendance at a *brit* stand before the "Throne of Elijah."

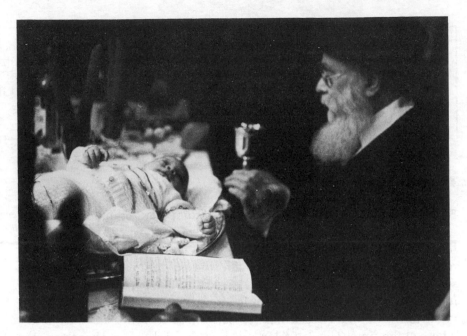

Why Elijah?

In the old days a charming custom placed a special chair at the *Brit* ceremony. It was called "the throne of Elijah" after Elijah the prophet, whose spirit was called upon to watch over and protect the newborn infant.

Why Elijah? Aside from his widespread folk popularity among the Jews of Eastern Europe, Elijah is known as the "angel of the covenant" (Malachi 3:1) because he defended the covenant before the priests of Baal on Mount Carmel. In this view every circumcision is a reenactment of Elijah's great affirmation of faith.

Another explanation is that Elijah was one of the sternest of the prophets, constantly criticizing the people of Israel for their wavering devotion to God. Later on, poetic justice demanded that Elijah return to earth to see just how universal was the Jewish acceptance of God's covenant.

Pidyon Ha-Ben

The ceremony of *pidyon ha-ben*—"redemption of the son"—takes place on the thirty-first day after the birth. *Pidyon ha-ben* only applies to a male who is his mother's first child. If her first child is a girl, the first-born boy is not "redeemed." It is the first-born of the mother who requires redemption, not of the father, so that if a man has male children by his first wife and his second wife has a male child, that child requires to be redeemed. The Torah, when speaking of *pidyon ha-ben* (Exodus 13:2), limits the ceremony to "the first issue of every womb." Furthermore, the same verse speaks of the Israelites. Consequently, there is no *pidyon ha-ben* if the father is a Cohen or a Levite or if the mother is the daughter of a Cohen or a Levite.

The reason given for *pidyon ha-ben* in the Torah is that because God slew the Egyptian first-born and spared the first-born of the Israelites, the first-born belong to God until they are redeemed. This is done by paying a Cohen (the priest who is God's representative) the sum of five silver shekels. Some historians find in the rite echoes of the very ancient custom in which the first-born of the family was a priest. The function of the priesthood was later given to Cohanim, the descendants of Aaron, brother of Moses, who are thus to be the agents through whom the redemption is carried out. There is the further idea that by dedicating the first-born in this way all the children born later are to carry on the Jewish tradition. The element stressed is dedication to God's service by the whole family.

The procedures for the ceremony are found in the prayer books. Here we need only give them in outline. The Cohen (anyone whose family has a tradition that they are Cohanim) asks the father which he would rather have, his first-born son or the five shekels. It is naturally unknown for a father to say he would rather have the shekels (it is not too fanciful to read into this custom the idea that, for Jews, children are a priceless gift). The father gives the five shekels to the Cohen, who then recites the priestly blessing over the infant. There is no certainty regarding the exact equivalent of five shekels in modern currency, so it is customary to give the Cohen a large amount of silver coins. The money belongs to the Cohen and should be given to him without reservation but if he so wishes he can return it to the father or give it to charity.

"The 'redemption of the son' ceremony stresses a family's dedication to God's service."

Bringing Up Children

Although a minor (a boy under the age of thirteen and a girl under the age of twelve) has no responsibility in Jewish law for what he or she does or fails to do, parents have the obligation to train their children in the Jewish way, both by direct teaching, according to their capacity to understand, and more significantly, by setting an example. Children should never be ordered by their parents to do wrong with the excuse that, after all, they are only children. But, by the same token, parents should not overburden their children with all the niceties of Jewish observance and should not present Judaism as merely a list of dos and don'ts. Untold harm is done by pious parents who threaten their children—"God will punish you if you do that"—as if God were a tyrant ready to pounce whenever His will is thwarted.

Parents have an obligation to train their children in the Jewish way.

Let them be Children

Scripture (I Samuel 1:24) states that when Hannah brought her little son to the House of God, "the child was young," which can be rendered as "and the child was childish." A Jewish preacher, Simeon Singer, remarked that Scripture advises us to acknowledge that children are children, not little adults. Their parents should not expect too much of them. They should be allowed to enjoy their youth while it lasts. Too often in the biographies of great rabbis tales are told of their precocity; they are described as little monsters of piety. It is as little fitting for a child to be grown up before his time as for an old man to be childish.

In most Jewish communities there are Jewish schools for the education of children in Judaism. Where no school is available parents should either teach their children themselves or arrange for private tutors. But there are whole areas of life in which, as has been said, religion must be *caught* not taught.

Boys Will Be Boys

A strain within Jewish folklore is fond of recording the antics of great scholars when they were ordinary little boys. A number of such stories are told about the great Lithuanian rabbi, Chaim Brisker, and his childhood friends.

One day Chaim came home with filthy hands. When his mother asked, "Did you ever see *me* with hands so dirty?" Chaim responded, "No, but *your* mother did."

On another occasion Chaim's father met the boy and his friend after a session at school. "So, boys," Chaim's father asked, "which one of you learned more today?"

Chaim thought for a moment. "I don't know what to say," he finally answered. "If I answer that I learned more, I'll be a braggart. If I say that my friend learned more, I'll be a liar."

To which his friend replied, "You're both."

Impress upon your Children

The Ḥafetz Ḥayyim once gave an interesting turn to the verses in the Shema (Deuteronomy 6:6–7): "Take to heart these instructions with which I charge you this day. Impress them upon your children. Recite them when you stay at home and when you are away, when you lie down and when you get up." According to the Ḥafetz Ḥayyim, this passage means: If you really want to impress your children with the teachings of Judaism then "recite them" yourselves, both at home and outside the home. When the children see that their parents love and follow the Jewish way, they too will be impressed and inspired to follow it.

Bar Mitzvah and Bat Mitzvah

A boy attains his majority at the age of thirteen, a girl at the age of twelve. At thirteen then the boy becomes responsible to keep the *mitzvot*. He becomes *bar mitzvah*, "a son of the *mitzvot*"—he belongs in the category of those obliged to perform the *mitzvot*. The girl becomes responsible too, at twelve; she becomes *bat mitzvah*, "a daughter of the *mitzvot*." We emphasize the word "becomes," since there is no need for any initiatory ceremony. It happens automatically. Nevertheless, in the Middle Ages, various special ceremonies were introduced for boys when they reached the age of bar mitzvah. The boy was called up to read a portion in the synagogue; a party was held to celebrate the event; he began to wear *tefillin*. (Minors did not wear *tefillin*, even though they were trained to keep the other *mitzvot* from an early age. Most little children, it was held, cannot be sufficiently clean in body and mind, the state required for the wearing of *tefillin*.) Nowadays, the celebration of the Bar Mitzvah is very well established, though the actual practices and ceremonies differ from community to community.

Bat Mitzvah ceremonies for girls are of more recent vintage, but have become increasingly popular. It is true that some Orthodox rabbis still object to these ceremonies as untraditional and therefore un-Jewish. However, since the Bar Mitzvah ceremonies are themselves an innovation it is hard to see why girls should be deprived if their own special occasion. The Bar Mitzvah ceremonies were also untraditional in the period when they were introduced. Not every effort at making Judaism more attractive must be rejected on the grounds that it has never been done before. In these matters, in any event, the family will be guided by the rabbi of the synagogue to which it is affiliated.

"Bat Mitzvah ceremonies for girls are of recent vintage, but have become popular."

8

Honoring Parents

Honor and Revere

Scripture uses two different expressions for the attitudes that children are expected to adopt towards their parents. In the fifth commandment (Exodus 20:12) the expression used is: "*Honor* thy father and thy mother"; whereas the expression used in Leviticus (19:3) is: "Each one of you shall *revere* his father and his mother."

On the basis of the two passages, the talmudic Rabbis teach that there is a double obligation: to *honor* parents and to *revere* them. The Rabbis note further that in the "honor" verse the father is mentioned first, in the "revere" verse the mother is mentioned first. The reason, according to the Rabbis, is that children are more ready to "honor" their mother than their father, but are more ready to "revere" their father than their mother (or, at least, that was the case in talmudic times). Consequently, the parent who might be neglected is mentioned first, as if to say, you may not need reminders to "honor" your mother and to "revere" your father, but do not forget to "honor" your father and to "revere" your mother. The Torah always stresses that which is less emphasized by human nature.

This is how the Rabbis spell out these two obligations: The duty to honor parents is defined as "Give your parents to eat and drink; clothe them; escort them in and out." The duty to revere parents is defined as: "Do not stand or sit in their place; do not contradict them; in

---

The Extent of Honoring Parents

Rabbi Tarfon had a mother for whom, whenever she wished to get in or out of bed, he would kneel down so that she could step on him. He went and boasted to his colleagues about how scrupulously he kept the fifth commandment. They said to him: "You have not done even the half required of you. When you see her take a purse of money and throw it into the sea, and you say nothing in objection, then you will have something to boast about."

Rabbi Assi had an old mother. She said to him: "I want some ornaments." So he had them made for her. She said to him: "I want a husband." He said: "I will look out for a husband for you." "I want a husband who is as handsome as you." He left her and went to the Land of Israel.

(*Babylonian Talmud, Kiddushin* 31b)

---

a dispute do not side with them, saying, 'My parent is right.' " The duty to honor parents is a positive one, to do that which they require; whereas the duty to revere is a negative injunction, not to do that which causes them distress.

Obligations of Children to Parents

These talmudic definitions require elaboration. For instance, to give parents food and drink, and to clothe them, can either mean that it is the duty of children to support their parents financially, or simply that children should be courteous to their parents, serving them with their meals and helping them on with their clothes when this is required, the food and clothing being purchased by the parents themselves. This question is debated by the later talmudic Rabbis. The final ruling is that children have no obligation to support their parents financially. Nevertheless, all concur that if the parents are too poor to provide for their own needs then their children must provide, even if they suffer heavy financial loss in the process.

That parents are not to be contradicted, nor to be patronized by children taking their part in a quarrel, does not mean that children may not disagree (or, for that matter, agree) with their parents. It only means that children should not give the impression of weighing and judging their parents' opinions in a superior and condescending manner. They are not bound, however, to forfeit their own opinions. Children have a right to their own views. Throughout the history of Jewish learning great scholars have disagreed with parents and teachers in their understanding of the Torah and have recorded their disagreement in the works they compiled. The fifth commandment does not demand any abandonment of the search for truth.

" 'Honor thy father and thy mother' (Exodus 20:12)."

"Children have a right to their own views."

"Nowhere is it suggested that children must admire their parents or even like them all the time."

The injunction against standing or sitting in the parent's place is taken both literally and figuratively. If a father has a special place at the head of the table or a favorite armchair in which he relaxes, the children should not sit in that place (unless, of course, the father has no objection). Figuratively, the injunction means that if a parent has a position in the community, for example, as a chairperson of an organization or as the director of a firm, children should not allow themselves to be elected to that position.

In these matters, however, and in all similar instances, parents can forgo their rights. It would be absurd for children to insist on paying tokens of honor to their parents if the parents do not want them to do so. For this reason, if parents want their children to call them by their first name, the children may do so. As one rabbi put it, in these and similar instances, to fall in with the wishes of parents is itself to honor them.

Some Limits

There are limits to what parents can legitimately demand of their children. The fifth commandment does not give *carte blanche* for parents to act as dictators. Children also have rights. It goes without saying that the wishes of parents should be disregarded if they order a child to commit a crime or disobey a religious law. (But Maimonides rules that even a parent who is a criminal or a sinner must still be honored and revered.) According to many authorities there is no obligation at all for children to obey their parents, other than in the cases mentioned above. Thus if parents object to the person their son or daughter wishes to marry, the parents' wishes are not necessarily to be respected. Naturally, children faced with this kind of problem will do their utmost to

win over their parents, but if they are unsuccessful they commit no wrong in following the dictates of their own heart.

When parents are divorced, children are often tempted to take sides, but they should resist the temptation. Children should avoid playing one parent against the other. When there are contradictory demands by the divorced parents—the father requesting one course of action, the mother another—the children, with an equal obligation to both, must do their best to be impartial without appearing to be wiser than their parents. This is not an easy path to follow.

It will be seen from all the above examples that the fifth commandment has more to do with correct behavior, which is controllable, than with emotions, which are not easy to control. Nowhere is it suggested, for instance, that children must admire their parents or even like them all the time. The honest way is for children to acknowledge hostile feelings toward their parents, where these exist, but to avoid, so far as possible, giving vent to these feelings in a way that will hurt the parents.

Extending the Fifth Commandment

The fifth commandment is extended by the Rabbis in a number of ways. Honor is to be paid, they say, to parents who are no longer alive. The institutions of *kaddish* and of Yahrzeit were introduced for this purpose. There are also other categories of persons to whom respect is due as an extension of the fifth commandment. These are grandparents, parents-in-law, step-parents, older siblings, teachers, and mentors. But since these are extensions of the fifth commandment, and respect for parents belongs to the original commandment, respect for parents always comes first. Where, for instance, the wishes of a grandparent conflict with those of a parent, the wishes of the parent take precedence.

Questions and Answers

Here are some examples of how these principles operate.

QUESTION

A young man wishes to study to become a doctor, but his father wishes him to give up his studies and join the family business. What should he do?

ANSWER

To obey the father in this instance is not part of the fifth commandment. The son should pursue his own career. But the son should be tactful. "I have set my heart on a career in medicine" is a correct response. "You don't imagine that I would think of joining a firm like yours" is the wong response and would be a breach of the fifth commandment.

"The son must never denounce his parents to the police."

The obligation to honor parents
does not end at death.

QUESTION

A young woman whose parents are not too careful about *kashrut* has
become very observant. She is invited to dine with her parents. Should
she refuse?

ANSWER

She should not refuse to eat in her parents' home since that would hurt
them. She should ask her mother to provide food she can eat—food that
would avoid doing violence to her conscience—but she should try to
be as lenient in her requirements as possible, forgoing the scrupulous-
ness she observes in her own home.

QUESTION

A son conducts a regular class in Talmud, which his father attends. Is
the son, as his father's teacher, exempt from keeping the fifth commandment?

ANSWER

Certainly not. As a scholar he ought to know that the fifth commandment is binding on all. Nevertheless, in these circumstances the father
should also pay special respect to his son as his teacher of the Torah.

QUESTION

A father visits his son's home. The son usually sits at the head of the
table. Is the son obliged to give up his seat at the head of the table to
his father?

ANSWER

It would be wrong for a son to take his father's place at the head of the table in the father's home. But in the son's home the son has no obligation to give up his special seat to his father.

QUESTION

A father has broken the law and his son knows of it. Should he report the father to the authorities?

ANSWER

The son must never do what the Nazis encouraged children to do, denounce their parents to the police. In fact, in Jewish law, the testimony of a son against his father (or of a father against his son) is never accepted by the court. The son may wish to compensate the victim of his father's crime, but that should be done in a way that will not humiliate the father.

9

Death and Mourning

Judaism has a realistic attitude towards death. On the one hand Judaism encourages mourning over the death of a near relative. Grief is to be expressed in a number of mourning rituals. On the other hand excessive mourning is frowned upon because that would suggest doubts about the way God orders His world. The authentic Jewish approach, difficult and heartrending though it is, is the cry of Job: "The Lord gave, and the Lord hath taken away; Blessed be the name of the Lord" (Job 1:21).

Maimonides on Mourning

"Let not a man mourn too much over a near relative who has departed this life, for that is the way of the world; it is stupid to grieve too much because the world is as it is. But whoever does not observe the mourning observances as laid down by the Sages is a cruel man."

Care For the Dying

A dying person must be left to die in peace. Nothing should be done to speed death, though a distinction is drawn in the sources between a positive act to hasten the end and the removal of something that prevents death. In the former case an act of taking life—albeit for humane reasons—is carried out, and that is forbidden. In the latter case it is permitted to take steps to remove the hindrance, even though the result will be a speedier death. It is not the act of removal that causes death. On the contrary, death comes naturally and it is only that which prevents death that is removed. Contemporary rabbis have discussed whether switching off a life-sustaining machine, to which a dying patient is attached, would fall under the heading of a positive act, and therefore be forbidden in Jewish law, or under the heading of a removal of a hindrance to dying, and therefore be permitted. There is no consensus on this question.

If the dying person is conscious, he should be told tactfully that it would be good to confess his sins before he dies. This suggestion should not be put to him in a brutal manner, as if it is certain that he

" 'The Lord gave, and the Lord hath taken away; Blessed be the name of the Lord' (Job 1:21)."

The members of a burial society take care of every aspect of the burial, from the moment of death to comforting the mourners. An illustration from an eighteenth-century book.

Membership in a burial society has always been a rare privilege. Burial Society Cup, Bohemia, 1692.

will die; he should be told instead that "many have confessed on their deathbed and yet have recovered." It rarely happens, in fact, that the dying are conscious just before the actual demise, but if they are they should, if they can, recite the Shema. Many are the tales of Jews who expired with "the Lord is One" on their lips, faithful to the very end.

Attending to the Body

After death the *taharah* ("purification rite") is carried out. In many communities this is attended to by a special brotherhood (for men) or sisterhood (for women) known as the Ḥevra Kaddishah, "Holy Society." Membership in the Ḥevra Kaddishah is considered to be a status symbol, a rare privilege given only to worthy members of the community. An interesting custom is the Ḥevra Kaddishah banquet, held on the seventh day of Adar, in celebration of their honorable activities.

Why on the seventh of Adar? This day is the traditional anniversary of the death of Moses. But the teachings of Moses still live on. Death was overcome on this day, so a celebration is in order for those who occupy themselves with the dead.

The *taharah* involves a thorough bathing and cleansing of the corpse. Although now lifeless, the body must be treated with respect. It was once a human being, a servant of God, created in His image. After the cleansing, the corpse is wrapped in shrouds (*takhrikhin*, from a root meaning "to wrap"). In ancient times, the Talmud observes that people sought to outdo one another in providing costly shrouds for their dead. This is said to have reached such a state that for the poor, the grief over the financial loss exceeded the grief over the lost relative. Consequently, the great and rich Rabban Gamaliel left in his will that he should be buried in shrouds made of plain linen. From his example, people took the lesson that if plain linen was good enough for Rabban Gamaliel it was good enough for all. It is now the universal Jewish custom to use shrouds of plain linen. All ostentation in these matters is inappropriate and extremely humiliating to those who can only afford a simple funeral.

It was debated, in the Middle Ages, whether a man should be buried in the *tallit* he wore during his lifetime. Some argued in favor, saying that a man's good deeds, represented by the *tallit*, should accompany him to his last resting place. Others disagreed. It is mocking the dead man, they argued, to provide him with a *tallit*, since the man is dead and can no longer carry out the *mitzvot*. In most communities a compromise is followed. The *tallit* is wrapped around the corpse after it is first rendered unfit by removing the *tzitzit* in one of the corners. Thus there is the reminder of his good deeds, but there is no mocking of the dead; the *tallit* is unfit for use.

Each stone represents a soul. The Jewish cemetery in Prague, Czechoslovakia.

Burial

Traditionally, burial must be in the earth in a Jewish cemetery. The old name for the cemetery is *Bet Olam* or *Bet Ha-Ḥayyim*, "The House of Eternity" or "The House of Life," a curious name for a cemetery. These might originally have been euphemisms, but they also denote that as Judaism understands it, death is not the end. The human soul is immortal.

Cremation is frowned upon by the tradition for a number of reasons. The most convincing of these are that the biblical heroes and heroines were buried in the ground, and that out of respect for the body, which once housed the soul, it should not actively be destroyed but left to come to dust. It is rather like a Sefer Torah no longer fit for use. It is not destroyed, but placed in the soil to fade away of its own accord.

It is forbidden to enjoy any benefit from a corpse or from anything appertaining to a corpse. But there is no basis for the widespread superstition that a man's shoes and clothes must not be worn by anyone else after his death.

A rite that is puzzling to some is that of washing the hands after the burial. One explanation is that the custom symbolically expresses the idea that life must go on. The realm of the dead is washed away, as it were; the hands return from burying the dead to engage in the activities of this world.

"It is the universal custom to use shrouds of plain linen. All ostentation is inappropriate."

The Tombstone

The old name for a tombstone is *nefesh*, meaning "soul." But the more usual name is the biblical *matzevah*, from a root meaning "to stand" (it "stands" in memory of the deceased). Customs vary as to when the stone is set. Some set the stone after eleven months, others earlier or later. In Israel the usual custom is to set the stone about a month after death. But there are no hard and fast rules about this.

At the Funeral

It is customary that the participants, first family then friends, throw three shovelfuls of earth upon the grave. The idea here is that each mourner has a share in the burial, a private moment of separation from the deceased.

Horizontal or Vertical

Sephardi tombstones are usually placed in a horizontal position, Ashkenazi stones in a vertical position. It is not clear why this variation developed. The Sephardim were probably influenced by the Islamic custom of horizontal stones, while the Ashkenazim were influenced by the differing Christian custom.

The Mourning Rites

"There is no reference to the dead in the Kaddish."

The mourning rites are observed by the seven nearest relatives of the deceased: father, mother, son, daughter, brother, sister, husband or wife. Brother and sister in this context mean even a half brother or half sister. Adopted children are not obliged to observe the mourning rites when their adopted parents die, but of course they may do so if they wish (as most do). The first of the mourning rites is carried out at the time of the funeral. This is *keriah*, "rending" the garment. The rending of garments as a sign of grief and mourning is mentioned in the Bible. There is no need to tear a jacket or dress—a cardigan or shirt will do. For parents the tear is made at the left side of the garment (nearest the heart), while for the other relatives it is made on the right side.

For seven days the mourners sit on low stools, and prayers are recited in the house of mourning. This is known as the *shivah* ("seven") or "sitting *shivah*." It is part of the *mitzvah* of *gemilut ḥas-adim* (mentioned in a previous chapter) to visit mourners and offer them words of comfort and consolation. Many people bring to the mourners gifts of food and drink. During the *shivah* the mourners should not attend their place of work or business. Lesser tokens of mourning, such as not listening to music, are observed for thirty days after the funeral. This is known as the period of *sheloshim*, or "thirty." For children mourning parents this mourning period lasts for a whole year.

Eleven Months

The *kaddish* is recited for eleven months after the death of a parent. Why only eleven? There is a talmudic statement to the effect that the wicked suffer in Hell for twelve months, other folk for less. Since the *kaddish* is said to assist the soul of the deceased parent to rise from Hell to Heaven (Judaism does believe in these, although interpretations differ as to what they mean), for a child to say the *kaddish* in the twelfth month is to imply that the parent is wicked and still awaits ascent to Heaven.

The Rebbe's Yahrzeit

Although traditionally the Yahrzeit is a sad occasion, the Ḥasidim observe the Yahrzeit of famous rebbes as an occasion for rejoicing, in the belief that on each Yahrzeit the saint ascends still higher in Heaven. Cakes and alcoholic drinks are provided and the blessing *Le-Ḥayyim* is given. In some non-Ḥasidic communities this custom has also caught on, people drinking *le-ḥayyim* on a Yahrzeit.

Kaddish and Yahrzeit

A son (and in some communities a daughter as well) recites the *kad-dish* ("sanctification") prayer in the synagogue for eleven months after the death of his (or her) parent. The custom of reciting the mourner's *kaddish* arose in medieval Germany and was at first observed only by

An ancient burial site reminds us that each generation attends to its dead. Bet Shearim, Israel.

the Ashkenazim, but it is now nearly universal. It has been noted often that there is no reference to the dead in the *kaddish*. As its name implies, the *kaddish* is a prayer for God's name to be magnified and sanctified in the world. When reciting the *kaddish*, one is saying: my parent lived as a Jew and thereby did something to sanctify God's name; so will I sanctify God's name in the synagogue and try to live as my parent did, sanctifying the Name through my daily living.

Where there are no children to recite the *kaddish*, it is often done by other relatives or by someone engaged to perform this duty.

The *Yahrzeit* (a German word meaning "anniversary") refers to the anniversary of the death of a loved one. It is observed by reciting the *kaddish* in the synagogue, by being called up to the Torah and reciting a prayer for the departed, and by kindling a *Yahrzeit* candle to burn throughout the twenty-four hours of the anniversary. The latter custom is based on the verse: "The spirit of man is the lamp of the Lord" (Proverbs 20:27). The custom of fasting on the anniversary of a parent's death is referred to in the Talmud. Very few follow this custom today.

10

The Dietary Laws

Kasher and Treyfah

Food permitted to be eaten according to the dietary laws is called *kosher* (in Sephardi and Israeli pronunciation *kasher*), while food forbidden by these laws is called *treyf* or *treyfah*. Both of these terms have an interesting etymology. The word *kasher* is found in the Book of Esther (8:4): "and the thing seems right (*kasher*) before the king." This word, then, simply means "right" or "correct," and originally was not applied especially to food. One can speak of a kosher Sefer Torah or a kosher *mezuzah*, meaning one fit and proper to be used, without defects. In rabbinic literature the term is used of human beings; one who behaves properly is called *adam kasher*, a kosher person.

The word *treyfah* occurs in the Book of Exodus (22:30) in connection with the dietary laws: "You shall be men holy unto Me: you must not eat flesh torn (*treyfah*) by beasts in the field, you shall cast it to the dogs." The Rabbis explain this passage as referring not only to the meat of an animal actually *torn* to death by wild beasts, but also to the meat of an animal with serious defects in its vital organs, from which it will eventually die. Later, the term *treyfah* was extended to all forbidden food.

In everday usage kosher food means food that may be eaten, and *treyfah* food means any food that may not be eaten, whatever the reason. Thus the cow is said to be a kosher animal and the pig a *treyfah* animal, even though the prohibition has nothing to do with an animal torn by wild beasts or having a disease of its vital organs. The abstract noun *kashrut* (from *kasher*) has now come to refer to the whole range of the dietary laws. One who keeps these laws is said to be observing *kashrut*.

It should also be noted that kosher is a negative term. It does not mean holy or good, but simply the absence of anything that might render food *treyf*. In other words, everthing is automatically kosher unless there is a law that declares it *treyf*. When potatoes were first brought to the West there was no need to find a special law concerning them. They can be eaten because none of the laws by which certain foods are forbidden has any possible application to potatoes. Nonkosher food, on the other hand, may be forbidden by one of the various dietary laws, not all necessarily of the same nature. Both pork

A highly qualified slaughterer, a *shohet*, is required to certify that food is kosher. Seal of the dietary law supervisor in a North African Jewish community.

and the meat of an animal with a defect in its vital organs are forbidden, but the two prohibitions are based on two diverse laws. The pig is not kosher because it belongs to the category of unclean animals, whereas the animal with the defect is not kosher because of the Exodus verse and its amplification in the rabbinic tradition.

What is Glatt Kosher?

One often sees food advertised as *Glatt Kosher*. The sense of this phrase is "extremely kosher," but strictly speaking, there can be no such thing. *Kashrut* admits no superlatives. Either a thing is kosher or it is not. Actually the term *glatt*, "smooth," referred to an animal whose lungs were "smooth," without adhesions, some of which may render the animal *treyfah*. Not wishing to mistake an adhesion that renders the animal *treyf* for one that does not, some extremely pious folk only ate the meat of animals with completely smooth lungs. Nowadays, the term *glatt* is extended to include all food that is very kosher, which, as we have seen, does not make much sense. Food that is *glatt kosher*, it can be safely assumed, has been prepared with great care to ensure that nothing *treyf* has been introduced. There is certainly no harm in such extra careful preparation, provided people do not use their practice to imply that the kosher food eaten by others is not really kosher.

Since ancient times Jews have asked: "Is it kosher?"

"One who behaves properly is called adam kasher, *a kosher person."*

Animals and Fishes

In the Torah (Leviticus, chapter 11, and Deuteronomy, chapter 14) the rules are laid down as to which animals, birds, and fishes may be eaten, and which may not.

With regard to animals and fishes, the Torah gives these indications: animals which chew the cud (ruminants) and have cloven hooves, and fishes which have fins and scales, are kosher. It is not clear, and the matter was discussed in the Middle Ages, whether these animals and fishes are kosher *because* of these characteristics (cud-chewing, cloven hooves, fins and scales) or whether these characteristics are only *indications* that the animals and fishes are kosher. It is impossible to know which view is correct since we are not told why some animals are kosher and others are not. Various reasons have been adduced: the hygienic reason (the pig, for instance, is a dirty animal harboring disease); associations with idolatrous practices; the need for the children of Israel to be separate in their eating habits from the pagans. But the Torah always stresses holiness as the ultimate reason for the dietary laws. The basic idea is that whatever the origin of these laws, obeying them promotes holy living. Jews who keep these laws introduce a spiritual element into their lives, even into the satisfaction of hunger, the most basic and animal-like of all human appetites. By means of the dietary laws one's everyday life becomes nobler and purer.

"The Torah always stresses holiness as the ultimate reason for the dietary laws."

Precise rules and requirements have been handed down from generation to generation.

Of animals the cow, the goat, the sheep, the deer, and the antelope are kosher, but the rabbit, the camel, the donkey, and the pig are not. Jews have always had such an abhorrence of the pig that many Jews, otherwise lax in their observance of the dietary laws, will not eat bacon or ham. It is not generally known that whale meat is not kosher, but not because it is a fish without fins and scales. Rather, it is an animal without cloven hooves and it does not chew the cud.

Birds

In contrast to the rules concerning animals and fishes, the Torah does not provide any indications to determine which birds are kosher and which are not. Instead the Torah lists all the forbidden birds. Since the birds in the list appear to be birds of prey, the prohibition may have something to do with an avoidance of anything that has associations with cruelty.

The implication of this list is that all other birds are kosher. Unfortunately, some of the birds in the list cannot be identified with any degree of certainty (the English translations are all based on conjecture). As a result, a bird can be eaten only if there is a tradition that it is kosher. Chicken, turkeys, and geese are kosher and are eaten by Jews everywhere. The eggs of nonkosher birds are forbidden on the principle "whatever comes from the unclean is unclean." It is not generally known, however, that quails are kosher and that it is permitted to eat quail eggs.

"It is believed that shehitah *is the least painful method used in killing animals."*

> ### Is Sturgeon Kosher?
>
> A fierce debate took place in the eighteenth century regarding the sturgeon, the source of caviar. Those who permitted it argued that the sturgeon has fins and scales and is consequently kosher. Those who declared it nonkosher held that it all depends on how one defines scales. The sturgeon's scales are so deeply embedded in the skin that they can only be removed with the greatest difficulty. Consequently they are not scales at all but part of the skin of the fish, and a fish without scales is not kosher.

Shehitah

Even a kosher animal may not be eaten unless it has been killed by the method known as *shehitah* (the word means "killing," that is, the killing of animals in the prescribed manner). *Shehitah* involves the killing of the animal by a qualified Shohet with a special knife containing not the slightest flaw. It is believed by observant Jews that *shehitah* is the least painful of methods used in killing animals for food. Moreover, through *shehitah*, the brutalization often resulting from killing for food is avoided. In premodern Europe, for example, a farm family might have decided to kill a chicken by wringing its neck. A Jewish family, bound by the laws of *Kashrut* and *shehitah*, could not have even thought of such an act.

A Crocodile Handbag?

Is it permitted to have a pigskin wallet or a crocodile handbag? The non-kosher animals, birds, and fishes may not be eaten, but it is permitted to enjoy other benefits from them. There is no objection to owning and using objects made from the pig, the crocodile, or any other nonkosher animal. This may seem strange to some, yet no one questions the use of silk even though the silkworm may not be eaten.

Kosher Bacon?

Is "kosher bacon"—that is, kosher food manufactured to look and taste like bacon—kosher? It involves no offense against the dietary laws to eat "kosher bacon" since, after all, the meat itself is kosher. Whether it is desirable or not is another matter. It can be argued that it is undignified for a Jew to eat anything resembling the abhorrent animal. If "kosher bacon" is eaten, care must be taken that people who witness it should know that the food is kosher. Otherwise they might think that real bacon is being eaten. It is wrong to give the impression of wrongdoing even though one is innocent of it. To give an example from the ethical sphere, an honest person should never allow people to imagine that he is resorting to cheating even though he himself knows that he is doing nothing dishonest. The standards must both be kept and *seem* to be kept.

Salting Meat

Blood of animals and birds must not be eaten. (This prohibition does not apply to the blood of fishes.) Even blood found in eggs is forbidden. The custom is, in fact, to throw away the whole egg, not only the blood spot.

The Blood Libel

Jews have always had the strongest aversion to imbibing blood, an aversion that makes nonsense out of the already nonsensical canard that Jews have used Christian blood in the preparation of *matzah* for Passover. The blood libel would be comical were it not for the tragedies it has produced.

There is a standard procedure, known as *meliḥah*, "salting," for removing as much blood as possible from the meat or fowl (removing all the blood is not possible and is therefore not required). The meat should first be soaked in water for half an hour. It is then salted (with salt neither too coarse nor too fine) over all its surface and left on a draining board for an hour. It is then rinsed free of salt and can be cooked. Nowadays, most kosher butchers sell meat that has already been salted in the proper way.

The liver contains so much blood that it is not salted but instead broiled over a naked flame. Strictly speaking, broiling is enough; no salting is required. But it is the custom to give the liver a token sprinkling of salt before broiling.

Meat and Milk

The Torah states three times (Exodus 23:19; Exodus 34:26; Deuteronomy 14:21): "You shall not boil a kid in its mother's milk." On the face of it this is an extremely puzzling rule. Who would want to do such a horrible thing? Perhaps the reference is to some ancient rite by means of which pagan idolaters sought to encourage the growth of their crops and the birth of their animals.

According to the rabbinic tradition, the rule covers not only boiling a kid in its mother's milk but the boiling of any meat in any milk. In the traditional view it is forbidden to cook meat and milk together. Later on, by rabbinic law, this prohibition was extended to eating meat and milk dishes at the same meal. Later on still, the law was introduced that dairy dishes should not be eaten after meat until a certain period of time has elapsed. The time for waiting has varied according to local custom. Some wait six hours, some three, and some only one. Meat may, however, be eaten after dairy dishes. (One reason given for the waiting period is that meat sticks to the teeth and may still be in the mouth when dairy dishes are eaten. By this same reasoning, meat may be eaten after dairy dishes without any time lapse.) It is customary, however, to wash the mouth out beforehand.

Various reasons have been given for the prohibition of meat and milk. Maimonides thinks it is because a mixture of meat and milk is heavy and indigestible, and that the practice of cooking meat in milk was a pagan practice to be avoided by the holy nation. Another suggestion that has been offered is that meat represents death (the animal is killed before the meat is eaten) whereas milk represents life. Life and death must be kept separate; death must not be allowed to encroach upon life. Others hold that the prohibition serves as a reminder to make distinctions in life, to keep apart things and ideas that have no connection with one another, so that our thinking is precise, logical, and wholesome.

> *" 'You shall not boil a kid in its mother's milk' (Exodus 23:19, 34: 26; Deuteronomy 14:21)."*

The Kabbalah on Meat and Milk

Why may meat be eaten after milk but not milk after meat? A kabbalistic reason is that red is the color of blood and war, and hence, of power and judgment; whereas milk is white, the color of purity and mercy. If milk is partaken of first and mercy established, then force and power have been softened with a softener; when mercy precedes justice, then justice is tempered with love. Not so when meat is eaten first, for then power predominates; justice without the capacity of love to control becomes power unrestrained.

Utensils

Dairy food should not be cooked in meat utensils, and vice versa. It is the usual practice in a Jewish home to have two complete sets of dishes and cutlery, one for meat and the other for milk. Meat dishes are known in Yiddish as *fleishig* ("meaty"). Milk dishes are known as *milchig* ("milky"). Food and utensils that are neither *fleishig* nor *milchig* are known as *parave* (a word of uncertain origin, pronounced *par-a-veh*). Sometimes these terms are applied figuratively to persons. A strong personality is said to be *fleishig*, a palid personality to be *milchig*, a neutral person ("neither fish nor fowl," an English speaker might say) is said to be *parave*.

Dishwashers

May one use the same dishwasher for *milchig* and *fleishig* dishes? Many au- thorities permit it, but not at the same time.

A pot in which *treyfah* food has been cooked must not be used for cooking kosher food even if it is thoroughly scoured. The principle is that a "taste" of the *treyfah* food remains in the walls of the pot. However, the pot can be made kosher by filling it with clean water and bringing it to a boil. If a utensil has been used for *treyfah* on a naked flame or in a fire, the method of rendering it kosher is to heat it thoroughly over a fire. The general principle is described as "it exudes (the *treyfah*) in the way it absorbs." China cannot be made kosher since this material is so thoroughly absorbant that no amount of *kashering* can get rid of the *treyfah*. Many contemporary authorities hold that Pyrex dishes, on the other hand, can be *kashered*.

Holiness is everywhere, including the kitchen. Hand-washing before the Sabbath meal in Amsterdam, Holland.

Neutralization

The general principle is that *treyfah* food becomes neutralized in a ratio of one to sixty. Thus if a very small piece of *treyfah* meat was cooked in a pot of kosher meat and can no longer be identified, then it is kosher, provided it has sixty times as much kosher meat as *treyfah*.

A further rule states that if food is cooked in a utensil that was used for *treyfah* more than twenty-four hours earlier, the food is kosher. The principle here is that when *treyfah* food has remained for twenty-four hours or more in a utensil, its taste becomes "flawed" and cannot then contaminate the food subsequently cooked in that utensil. But doesn't this principle eradicate the need for keeping separate dishes for meat and milk? Why not have the same dishes for both and simply wait twenty-four hours between use for meat and use for milk? The answer is that both the principle of neutralization and the principle of "flawed" *treyfah* only operate as *faits accomplis*—when meat and milk have come in contact inadvertently. By rabbinic law it is not permitted to cook kosher food in a *treyfah* pot or meat in a milk pot. Nor is it permitted to put a small quantity of *treyfah* food into a dish of kosher food or a small quantity of milk into a meat dish. The reason why the Rabbis do not allow all this is because it would lead, eventually, to complete disregard of the laws regarding *treyfah* and meat and milk. However, if such accidents do unintentionally occur, it is permitted to neutralize them in the manner described.

Send the Other Chicken

A little girl came to a rabbi with a chicken. She said: "My mother sent me to ask you if this chicken is kosher." "Go home," said the rabbi, "and tell your mother to send the other chicken." The mother was astonished that the rabbi could have known that she had an-other chicken. "Elementary," replied the rabbinic detective. "The chicken brought to me by the little girl had nothing whatever wrong with it. The mother would not have asked a *shaylah* about such a fowl. I concluded therefore that she sent me the wrong chicken."

Asking a Shaylah

Actually the Hebrew word for a "question" should be pronounced *she-e-lah* (accent on the last syllable), but the Yiddish form, *shaylah*, has come to stay. Since the laws of neutralization, about "flawed" food, and about which defects render a fowl *treyfah* and which do not, are extremely complicated, one is advised to consult a rabbi whenever there is doubt (when a meat pot has been stirred with a milk spoon, for example). This is called: "asking a *shaylah*"—putting the question to a rabbi. The rabbi, expert in these matters, will examine the case and decide whether or not the food is permitted.

11

The Sabbath

"Remember" and "Keep"

There are two versions of the fourth commandment: "*Remember* the Sabbath day" (Exodus 20:8) and "*Keep* the Sabbath day" (Deuteronomy 5:12). In the rabbinic tradition these two expressions—*remember* and *keep*—refer to the positive and negative aspects of Sabbath observance. *Remembering* the Sabbath means reciting the *kiddush* ("sanctification") over a cup of wine; it also embraces the need to preserve the special Sabbath atmosphere of rest and tranquility. *Keeping* the Sabbath means refraining from work on that day.

"Work" in this context, according to the traditional view, does not necessarily mean excessive manual effort, but rather any act through which human beings exercise creative control over nature. Moving heavy objects around the house, for example, is not a creative manipulation of nature and hence does not fall under the heading of "work" (though it would surely offend against the "rest" principle). Writing, on the other hand, although comparatively effortless, does fall under the heading of "work," since it is a creative act. Many commentators have seen in all this the idea that by refraining from creative activity on the Sabbath, Jews acknowledge God as Creator, Whose gifts of creativity are given to humans during the six days of the week not by right but by permission.

"Come, let us welcome Queen Sabbath." (Rabbi Hanina ben Hama, Talmud)

74

Refraining from Work

Whole volumes have been written on the types of "work" forbidden on the Sabbath. Here we refer to some of them. In the Mishnah, the entire tractate Shabbat, comprising 157 huge double pages, is devoted to the theme. It lists the types of work forbidden. Here are some of those with direct application today: baking, cooking, and making fire; writing, drawing, and painting; pruning trees, cutting flowers, and gardening in general; carpentry, pottery making, and any kind of construction work; weaving, knitting, and embroidery; hunting and fishing; and all business activity. To smoke on the Sabbath involves kindling fire, as does the striking of a match.

Games which involve no infringements of the laws about "work" are allowed on the Sabbath. Examples are: card games, chess, billiards, ping-pong, scrabble (to put the letters together to form words does not constitute "writing"), and ball games in one's own home. When playing games on the Sabbath there must be no writing down of the score and no playing for money.

"On the Sabbath, Jews acknowledge God as Creator, Whose gifts of creativity are given to humans not by right but by permission."

We are commanded to study Jewish texts on the Sabbath.

Muktzeh

A rabbinic extension of the Sabbath prohibitions is known as muktzeh ("that which is set aside"). This means that objects normally used for activities proscribed on the Sabbath should not be handled. If one were to handle a saw, for example, one might easily forget that it is the Sabbath and use it to saw some wood. Other examples of muktzeh are pens and pencils, money, matches, and every kind of tool used normally for "work" within the Sabbath definition of the same. Muktzeh may, however, be handled if the place where it rests is required for other purposes. If there are pens and pencils on a table that has to be set for a meal, they may be removed from the table.

"Whole volumes have been written on the types of 'work' forbidden on the Sabbath."

Modern Times

In modern times, two acute problems have arisen in connection with Sabbath observance: traveling by car and using electricity. Orthodox rabbis hold that both these activities are not permitted on the Sabbath, but many Conservative rabbis do permit both the switching on of electric lights and the use of a car to attend synagogue, for those worshipers who live too far to go by foot.

When electricity was first harnassed for use, some Orthodox rabbis advanced the theory that to switch on an electric light does not break the commandment against kindling fire. They reasoned that there is no combustion in the filament, and kindling without combustion does not fall under the heading of "kindling" as defined by the Sabbath laws. When a light switch is pressed, these rabbis argued, no fire is kindled; all that happens is that a current flows through the wires. So the act of switching on the light is very different from a direct kindling of fire. But the opposite opinion has won out among Orthodox Jews, and today most Orthodox Jews have a timer to regulate the electric lights automatically. No one suggests that to set the timer before the Sabbath is in any way wrong.

Sabbath Delight

In addition to "remembering" and "keeping" the Sabbath, the Rabbis derive further Sabbath ideas from the verse in the Book of Isaiah (58: 3): "If thou turn away thy foot because of the Sabbath, From pursuing thy business on My holy day; And call the Sabbath a delight, And the holy of the Lord honorable, And shall honor it, not doing thy wonted ways, Not pursuing thy business, nor speaking thereof." The two basic ideas derived from the verse are: *oneg shabbat* ("Sabbath delight") and *kavod shabbat* ("Sabbath honor," paying special honor to the day). The Sabbath is to be treated as a day of delight (in this context, quiet enjoyment) and a day to be welcomed and treated as an honored guest. Jews wear special Sabbath clothes ("the sabbath best"); eat special meals (one on Friday night and two during the day); walk tranquilly and unhurriedly (unless one enjoys running as sport); take time for prayer and for study of the Torah; spend time with one's family; banish care and worry so far as possible; and bathe on the eve of the Sabbath so as to enter the Sabbath well-groomed. In furtherance of these ideas, cheerful songs—*zemirot*—are sung at the Sabbath table.

> *"Two acute problems have arisen in connection with Sabbath observance: traveling by car and using electricity."*

God's Business

The Rabbis note that the verse (Isaiah 58:13) says that the Sabbath should be a day of "not pursuing *thy* business, nor *speaking* thereof." It is only *thy* business that should not be done. God's business may be done; one can make calculations for charity or for the synagogue chest. Furthermore, since the verse refers to "*speaking* thereof," it is only to speak of business that should be avoided. It would be asking too much for a person not to *think* of business during the whole of the Sabbath.

Question:

Is it permitted to weep on the Sabbath?

Answer:

Since the Sabbath is to be a day of delight, weeping is hardly conducive to to the Sabbath spirit. But the Rabbis were realistic in their assessment of human nature. If, they say, someone has received some bad news and needs to find relief in tears, it would be cruel to expect that person to bottle up natural feelings. The relief afforded by weeping, say the Rabbis, is that person's *oneg shabbat!*

The Procedures in the Home

Before the Sabbath commences, the wife lights two candles in honor of the day: one to represent the injunction, "remember the Sabbath," the other to represent, "keep the Sabbath." After she has lit the candles she recites the benediction, "Who has commanded us to kindle the Sabbath lights," and prays for the well-being of her husband and family. Some people add more candles so that there is a candle for each member of the family. The *mitzvah* of kindling the Sabbath lights is particularly the wife's. But if there is no woman in the household the candles should be kindled by the oldest man present.

Normally a benediction over the performance of a *mitzvah* is recited before the *mitzvah* is performed. The reason why this benediction is recited afterwards is that saying it indicates an acceptance of Sabbath rest. It is then incorrect to kindle a fire.

"Remember the Sabbath day, to keep it holy." (Exodus 20:8)

Preparing the Table

The table is laid with a white tablecloth upon which are placed two loaves covered by a cloth (frequently embroidered with Hebrew words expressing the sanctity of the day), and cups (often of silver) for the wine over which *kiddush* is recited. Like the two candles, the two loaves correspond to "remember" and "keep," but they also represent the double portion of the Manna provided for the Sabbath in the wilderness (Exodus 16:22–26).

These loaves are called *ḥallot* (*challes* in Yiddish), a word meaning "loaves." Some people prefer to bake their own *ḥallot* in honor of the Sabbath. But any two loaves may be used, even two *matzot*, provided they are both whole. Here the symbolism is that the whole is always preferable to the incomplete. A person should have no reservations about Judaism, but should serve God wholeheartedly.

Two reasons are given for covering the loaves. First is that the Manna was covered by the dew (Exodus 16:13–14). The second is that *kiddush* is recited first and it is unfitting for the bread to be exposed

"The two loaves represent the double portion of manna *provided for the Sabbath in the wilderness."*

when it is not being used and a "rival"—the wine—is being used for the *kiddush*. This is a typically Jewish idea, of extending the idea of fairness even to inanimate things. The bread is covered so that it is not openly rejected in favor of the wine. If, however, wine is not available, or if one is not allowed to drink wine for health reasons, the *kiddush* can also be recited over the two loaves.

Blessing the Children

Before the *kiddush* is recited the father places his two hands on the heads of his children and blesses each of them in order of age. The blessing to boys is based on the story of Jacob blessing his grandsons (Genesis 48:20): "God make you as Ephraim and Manasseh." For girls the blessing is: "God make you as Sarah, Rebekah, Rachel, and Leah." The priestly blessing (Numbers 6:22–27) is also recited. Although the priestly blessing may only be recited by Cohanim during synagogue worship, it is recited by any parent, Cohen or not, on Sabbath eve at home. The priestly blessing is followed by the praise of the woman of worth (Proverbs, chapter 31) which is recited or sung in honor of the wife and mother (if she is present).

"May the Lord make His face shine upon you and be gracious unto you." (Numbers 6:25, and part of the blessing for children recited Sabbath eves at home.) Sculpture by Walter Midener, 1956.

Kiddush

The *kiddush* consists of the verses in the creation narrative (Genesis 2:1–3) describing how God completed His work and rested on the Sabbath, hence consecrating the Sabbath. In addition to these verses there are two benedictions: one over the wine and the other praising God for giving Israel the Sabbath. *Kiddush* is recited over wine because wine "gladdens the heart" (Psalm 104:15). The rituals of Judaism should be carried out in a spirit of joy, not as a burden unwillingly carried. All those present drink of the wine. The hands are then ritually washed with water from a glass or cup, first poured twice over the right hand and then twice over the left. The blessing over the loaves is then recited and a piece of the bread is dipped in salt and given to each of those present. The meal is then served during which the *zemirot* are sung. After the meal a Sabbath grace is recited.

Sabbath Witness

The *kiddush* is recited while standing. It is a tremendous witnessing of God's creative activity. In Jewish law, witnesses to an event are required to give their evidence while standing, not sitting; because of the seriousness of the occasion the witnesses stand to attention.

Two meals are eaten during the day. The first, after the morning synagogue service, is also preceded by *kiddush* (a shorter version than the Friday night *kiddush*), consisting of other Scriptural verses on the Sabbath theme (Exodus 31:16–17) and the blessing over wine. For this *kiddush* it is not necessary to have wine. Other alcoholic drinks are in order. This meal, too, should be preceded by the blessing over two whole loaves.

For the third meal of Sabbath, the second of the day, taken in the afternoon, it is not essential to have a full meal. Cakes and coffee will suffice, though many pious Jews have the two loaves for this meal as well and eat at least a little bread.

Between Sacred and Profane

At the termination of the Sabbath, the *havdalah* ("division") is recited, in which God is praised for making "distinctions"—between the sacred and the profane, between light and darkness, between Israel and other nations, between the seventh day and the six workdays. *Havdalah*, too, should be recited over wine or other alcoholic beverages (or even, according to many authorities, nonalcoholic drinks). The Sabbath is now over, so a Havdalah candle can be kindled. God is then praised for giving humans the great gift of fire and light. Since the benediction is one of thanks for "fire" it is not recited over a single candle but over two or more placed together. It is customary to use a special Havdalah candle in which there are a number of thin candles plaited together with a number of wicks. It is customary to extend the fingers toward the light. Two reasons are given in the sources. First, some use should be made of the "fire" while thanking God for it; the use here is that of distinguishing between light and shadow on the hands. Secondly, it is to denote that the hands, restricted from doing work on the Sabbath, can now be extended in labor.

It is also proper, at the Havdalah ceremony, to smell sweet spices or perfume. A beautiful rabbinic saying has it that on the Sabbath the Jew acquires an additional soul. When the Sabbath departs, this soul departs with it; the fragrant spices are smelled to refresh the soul.

Kiddush cup sculpted in silvered-bronze by Hana Geber.

A Ḥasidic master once said: "I know that Elijah cannot come on the Sabbath because he is not allowed to travel on the sacred day. Yet, as a rabbi, I give him a dispensation to travel, since if only he will come many lives will be saved; the coming of the Messiah will mean an end to war. I take full responsibility: the saving of life takes precedence over the Sabbath. So he can come and need not worry about any desecration of the Sabbath."

At the termination of the Sabbath, we thank God for making distinctions—the distinction between light and darkness, the distinction between holy and profane.

Melave Malka

"On the Sabbath the Jew acquires an additional soul."

Some Jews, especially the Ḥasidim, hold an additional festive meal on Saturday night. This is the *Melave Malka.* Originally this term meant "escorting the king," but later it came to mean "escorting the queen." When a royal guest has visited a home the guest is treated to a farewell meal before departure; so it is with the departure of Queen Sabbath. The Ḥasidim use the occasion to tell tales of the Ḥasidic masters. There are songs for the termination of the Sabbath, among them the well-known song about Elijah the prophet. Elijah, the herald of the Messiah, cannot travel until the end of the Sabbath, so he cannot bring his message that the Messiah is coming until Havdalah concludes. Consequently, this pleasant piece of folklore has it that as soon as the Sabbath is over, we invite Elijah to come.

Passover

Ḥametz and Matzah

Ḥametz is leavened bread, bread that has been allowed to rise ad become fermented. *Matzah* is unleavened bread, break baked before the dough has had time to rise and become fermented. There are complicated rules regarding what constitutes "rising" in this context. That is why during Passover, when it is forbidden to eat ḥametz, one may only eat foods containing grain if those foods have a *hekhshar*, a declaration from a competent rabbinic authority that they are kosher for Pesah—that is, completely free of ḥametz.

Except at the Seder, on the first night, there is no obligation to eat *matzah* specifically. All that is required is to abstain from eating ḥametz. No wrong is done if one goes through the rest of the festival without eating either ḥametz or *matzah*. This is how the majority of the codifiers understand the law: The Talmud states that while there is an obligation to eat at least a small amount of *matzah* on the first night, during the remainder of Passover *matzah* is *reshut* ("optional").

The great Gaon of Vilna argued otherwise. According to this eighteenth-century teacher, by "optional" the Talmud means that there is no *obligation*, as there is on the first night. No wrong is committed if *matzah* is not eaten during the remainder of Passover, but if *matzah* is eaten a *mitzvah* is performed. It is said that the Gaon was so convinced of the correctness of his opinion that not only would he eat *matzah* at every meal during Passover but he would recite the blessing (as we do on the Seder night): "Blessed art Thou, who has *commanded us* to eat matzah."

> " 'Leaven shall not be found in your houses for seven days' (Exodus 12:9)."

A Small Difference That Counts

It has been pointed out that the Hebrew letters of ḥametz and matzah are identical, except that ḥametz has a ḥet and matzah has a hey. The difference between these letters is very small. Often the difference between right and wrong is very little, but it is this very little that counts.

The search for *ḥametz* involves going through the house with a candle and examining all the rooms. An eighteenth-century drawing by Bernard Picart.

The Search For Ḥametz

Ḥametz is different from all other forbidden foods in that it must be removed from the house before Passover. "Leaven shall not be found in your houses for seven days" (Exodus 12:19). At all other times there is no harm in keeping nonkosher food in the house, provided one does not eat it. One of the reasons *ḥametz* is treated so much more strictly is that one is used to eating it during the rest of the year. If it were allowed to keep *ḥametz* in the house during Passover one could easily forget that it is Passover and eat the *ḥametz* as one does during the rest of the year.

It is only *ḥametz* belonging to a Jew that must not be kept in the house. Ḥametz belonging to a non-Jew (who, naturally, is under no obligation to keep Passover) may be kept in the house. If, for example, there is a non-Jewish guest or resident in the house, he can have as much *ḥametz* in his room as he wishes without the Jewish owner of the house committing any offense.

On the night before Passover the house is searched to see whether there is any *ḥametz* in the rooms. If *ḥametz* is found it is put in a safe place until the morning, when it is removed from the house. Some say the correct procedure is to burn it if possible. Yet, just in case any *ḥametz* has been overlooked and is still in the house, a declaration is made to the effect that any *ḥametz* remaining in the house is rendered "as the dust of the earth." Through this declaration (found in the Passover Haggadah) the owner of the house declares that he abandons his ownership of any *ḥametz* remaining inside. It then becomes ownerless *ḥametz*, and as *ḥametz* that does not belong to a Jew, it may be kept in the house.

The search for *ḥametz* involves going through the house with a candle and examining all the rooms. All the *ḥametz* that is found is

"On the night before Passover, the house is searched to see whether there is any ḥametz *in the rooms."*

kept in a safe place in the breakfast room. From this, breakfast can be had if desired, but whatever is left should be destroyed.

Some people follow the practice of placing ten small pieces of ḥametz around the house to be "found" during the search. Their reasoning is that otherwise ḥametz might not be found and, if that happens, the blessing, "who has commanded us to remove ḥametz," will have been in vain. (It is wrong to recite a pointless blessing since to do so is to take God's name in vain.)

Others argue that it is better not to leave pieces of bread around the house just so that the blessing will not be said in vain. According to this argument the blessing does not refer to finding ḥametz but to searching for it and destroying it *if found*. It is the search that is the *mitzvah*, and since the search does take place there is no vain blessing. In this matter, local custom is followed. Where there is no local custom one can please oneself.

From the Kabbalah

According to the Kabbalah there are ten powers, or *Sefirot*, by means of which God becomes manifest in the universe. The ten pieces of bread left around the house before the search for *ḥametz* are said to correspond to these ten *Sefirot*.

The Sale of Ḥametz

It is no great hardship to remove all bread, cakes, pastas, and other ḥametz from the house before Passover, giving them away, for example, to non-Jewish friends. But people may have large quantities of whiskey, which is made from fermented grain and is therefore a mixture of ḥametz and water. And what is a Jewish shopkeeper to do with large quantities of ḥametz in his store? Surely, it cannot be expected that he get rid of his entire stock of ḥametz before Passover. This problem became especially acute in Russia and Poland, where a large number of Jews were inkeepers. In response to their cry for help, the rabbis introduced the formal sale of ḥametz, still practiced by many today.

The procedure is to sell (in a properly drawn up bill of sale) all the ḥametz to a non-Jew. (Nowadays this is usually done by a rabbi who is given power of attorney to act on behalf of others.) The non-Jew puts down a small deposit and then, according to Jewish law, the ḥametz belongs to him. Even though everybody knows quite well that the ḥametz will be returned to its Jewish owner after Passover, at the time the sale is perfectly valid and unconditional. The non-Jew is legally entitled to keep the ḥametz he has bought, although it is virtually certain that he will not do so.

The ḥametz that is sold should be kept in a locked cupboard during the whole of Passover. The bill of sale, in fact, specifies that the area of the house on which the ḥametz rests is also sold to the non-

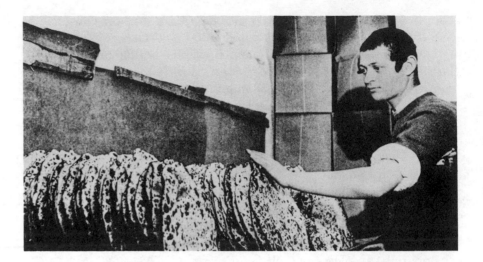

Since ancient times, the baking of *matzah* has been essential to the commemoration of the Exodus from Egypt.

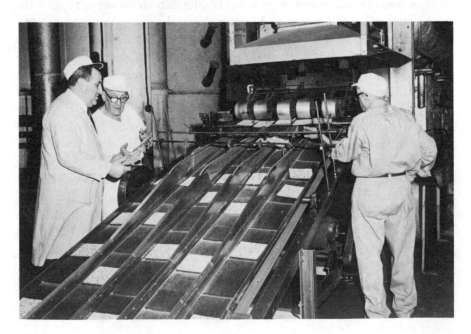

Jew so that he can keep his *ḥametz* there. In reality, it is not even *ḥa-metz* of a non-Jew in a Jewish house but *ḥametz* belonging to a non-Jew in his own domain.

Some people frown on the sale of *ḥametz* as a subterfuge, an attempt to fool God. But this is to misunderstand the nature of the whole exercise. Keeping *ḥametz* in the house on Passover is a religious, not an ethical, offense. If the religious law says that *ḥametz* belonging to a non-Jew may be kept in the house, what wrong is there in making such an arrangement beforehand? Using legal fictions to avoid ethical responsibilities and obligations is certainly unworthy of Jews. But using them for the purpose of keeping the religious law rather than simply ignoring it, as in the case of the sale of *ḥametz*, is not unworthy at all. It is an attempt not to trick God but to obey His law where the alternative would result in disobedience.

Fast of the First-Born

The last of the ten plagues was the slaying of the Egyptian first-born. The first-born of the Israelites were saved from destruction. (Vindictiveness is not a Jewish vice; there should be no gloating over the death of the Egyptian first-born. On the contrary, Scripture says that the first-born of the Israelites were "saved," seeming to imply that they were spared not because they deserved to be but rather as an act of divine mercy.

In post-talmudic times, it became the custom of many first-born to fast on the eve of Passover in recognition of God's merciful sparing the Israelite first-born. Even now, some first-born fast on this day. The more usual practice, however, is for the first-born to attend what is known as a *siyyum*. A *siyyum* ("ending") is the completion of a whole tractate of the Talmud. Whenever a scholar completes a tractate he invites his friends to a small celebration. So important is it to rejoice with the scholar who has mastered a sizable amount of Torah learning that the *mitzvah* of celebrating with him overrides any fast that people would otherwise have undertaken. Thus in Orthodox synagogues, the rabbi, or another scholar, completes his tractate (having studied it during the year) and the first-born participates in the celebration, breaking his fast. An incidental bonus is that the first-born has a taste not only of the food and drinks provided but also of Jewish learning.

"It became the custom of many first-born to fast on the eve of Passover in recognition of God's merciful sparing of the Israelite first-born."

The Seder

The details of the Seder on the first night of Passover are in all the numerous editions of the Passover Haggadah and do not require repetition here. We refer in this section only to the somewhat less familar aspects of the Seder.

The word Seder means "order"—the procedures adopted for the celebration. The purpose in ordering a celebration is to create a certain

*"All good Jewish
learning proceeds by
question and answer."*

atmosphere. One arrangement of the material serves one particular purpose; for a different purpose, a different order would be necessary. For instance, the Rabbis remark that there is no chronological order to Scripture. But there is an ordering of the material so as to convey a different message. Indeed, some of the sequence of the Seder is consciously designed to be "out of order," precisely because this will awaken the curiosity of children and interest them in the four questions. All good Jewish learning proceeds by question and answer.

The table should be laid beforehand with all the requirements for the Seder. These are placed on a large Seder dish (known as the *kaarah*, "dish"), often decorated with Passover symbols. There should be three whole *matzot*, bitter herbs, *ḥaroset*, salt water, *karpas*, a roasted bone, and a roasted egg.

Seder **means order—the procedures adopted for the celebration.**

Leḥem Oni

The three *matzot* are said to correspond to the threefold division among Jews—Cohanim, Levites, and Israelites. Another reason for the three *matzot* is that the blessing over the *matzah* should be over a whole *matzah* (wherever possible God is to be thanked over a loaf that is complete). Another whole *matzah* is required for the remembrance of Hillel, adding up to two *matzot*, both whole. Why the third? *Matzah* is described in the Torah as *leḥem oni*, translated as "bread of the poor." The poor rarely have a whole loaf. They often have to be content with a morsel. Consequently, the middle *matzah* is broken into two pieces, one of these hidden away to be used at the end of the meal for the *afikoman*, the other serving as the less than whole loaf that is typical of "bread of the poor." The blessing over the *matzah* is thus made over the whole *matzah* (so that there is the required wholeness) and over the broken piece of the middle *matzah* (so that there is the required "bread of the poor"). A piece of each of these is distributed to the participants. Hence there are three *matzot*: a whole one for the blessing, another whole one for "Hillel," and a third for the *afikoman* and the "bread of the poor."

Horseradish is often used for the bitter herbs, but lettuce can also be used. Although lettuce is not bitter, its roots are, and they qualify it as "bitter herbs." The ḥaroset is a paste used as a sauce into which the bitter herbs are dipped. It is made of sweet things and so symbolizes the way God brought joy and redemption out of the bitterness of Egyptian bondage. The ḥaroset is usually made of apples, almonds and cinnamon, the whole mixed with wine to form a thick mixture.

Salt water on the seder plate denotes the bitterness, the tears, of the Egyptian bondage.

Karpas

The salt water is to denote the bitterness, the tears, of the Egyptian bondage. The *karpas* can be any vegetable, but generally cucumber or parsley is used. According to one interpretation the word means "green," as is perhaps suggested in the story of the hangings in the king's palace (Esther 1:6): "White, green (*karpas*) and purple." The reason for the *karpas* is that in ancient times it was always the practice to eat something dipped in a sauce or liquid before the meal, much as today we often dip pieces of raw vegetables into a dip. To the *karpas* dip before the meal, the Rabbis added a second: the dipping of the bitter herbs into ḥaroset. Their purpose was that children, noticing this second dip, would ask about it. Originally, the fourth question was: "On all other nights we only dip once; on this night twice." But later, in Western lands, where there was no dipping at all, the question was altered to: "On all other nights we do not even dip once; on this night we dip twice."

Both the roasted egg and the bone are a reminder of the two sacrifices brought on Passover in Temple times. The paschal lamb was eaten roasted, the ḥagigah (from ḥag, "festival") was offered on each festival, and the pesaḥ, or paschal lamb, was offered only on Passover.

Conducting the Seder

A well-known form found in the Haggadah—*kadesh u-reḥatz*—was compiled to assist the leader conducting the Seder. Here we examine each of the terms in the order in which they appear.

1. *Kadesh*: recite the *kiddush* over a cup of wine, the first of the four cups to be drunk during the Seder. The number four features prominently in the Seder—the four cups of wine, the four sons, the four questions. One reason given in the Talmud for the four cups is that these correspond to the four different expressions used for redemption in the Exodus narrative (Exodus 6:6–7).

┌─ Four Cups ────────────────────────────

Another reason given for drinking four cups of wine at the Seder is that the word "cup" occurs four times in the story of Joseph's interpretation of the chief cupbearer's dream (Genesis, chapter 40). What is the connection? If Joseph had not interpreted the dream correctly he would not have risen to power; his father and brothers would not have settled in Egypt; there would have been no Egyptian bondage and no Exodus. Apparently insignificant events often have huge consequences.

---

2. *U-reḥatz*: wash the hands. In ancient times, whenever something was dipped in liquid there was a ritual washing of the hands. Nowadays, except at the Seder, there is only a ritual washing be-

Silver seder plate from Vienna, 1815. Sculpted human figures hold containers for the Passover symbols above a three-tiered plate for the three whole *matzot*.

fore eating bread. This is one of the ancient customs that has dropped out of Jewish life. But at the Seder, which has its origin in ancient procedures at meals, the washing has been retained.

3. *Karpas*: partake of the greens dipped in salt water.

4. *Yaḥatz*: break in two. The middle *matzah* is broken into two pieces. One of these is hidden, to be taken out at the end of the meal for use as the *afikoman*. There are many interpretations of this word. The most convincing is that it is a Greek word for dessert taken at the end of a meal. In Temple times no dessert was served, the paschal lamb itself being the *afikoman*, the dessert, so that its taste, and not the taste of any other food, would remain on the palate. After the destruction of the Temple this could not be done. Eventually, as a reminder, the piece of *matzah* eaten at the end of the meal became the *afikoman*.

5. *Maggid*: telling the story of the Exodus. The word Haggadah means "the telling." The Passover Haggadah contains the story to be "told," together with various rabbinic elaborations. The "telling" is in response to the four questions, usually asked by the youngest child present.

"The word Haggadah *means 'the telling.' The Passover Haggadah contains the story to be told."*

6. *Raḥatzah*: washing. The second ritual washing of the hands before eating *matzah*.

7. *Motzi*: The blessing over bread is recited—"Blessed art Thou, O Lord our God, who brings forth (*ha-motzi*) bread from the earth."

8. *Matzah*: The blessing over the *matzah* is recited—"Blessed art Thou, O Lord our God, who sanctified us with His commandments and commanded us to eat *matzah*."

9. *Maror*: bitter. The bitter herbs are dipped in the *ḥaroset* and eaten.

10. *Korekh*: binding. A "sandwich" is made of two pieces from the bottom *matzah* (the top two have been used by now), filled with some bitter herbs and *ḥaroset*, and eaten. This is said to be in memory of Hillel, who, in Temple times, would eat some of the paschal lamb, the *matzah*, and the bitter herbs at the same time.

Hillel is one of the best-known of the ancient Sages. Everyone has heard of his saying: "If I am not for myself who is for me? But if I am only for myself what am I?"

Ḥad Gadya

Rabbi Isaac Shapira of Slonim rebuked a man in his community who was always running people down. The rabbi said that the kid (in the *Ḥad Gadya*) was innocent, so the "cat that bit the kid" was wrong. Now if the cat was wrong, the "dog that bit the cat" was right. It follows that the stick was wrong, the fire right, the water wrong, the ox right, the *shoḥet* wrong, and the angel of death right. But if the angel of death was in the right, why did God slay the angel of death? The answer, said the Rabbi, is that even when one is in the right one must never be an "angel of death."

---

11. *Shulḥan Arukh*: arranged table. (The name, incidentally, of the great code of Jewish law compiled in the sixteenth century by Rabbi Joseph Karo.) There are many different customs as to the dishes eaten at the Seder meal. Many communities include hard-boiled eggs with salt water. Two reasons have been given for the custom. First, the obvious one, is that the hard-boiled egg represents the hard and cruel bondage suffered by the Israelites in Egypt. Secondly, eggs are a mourner's food. They are oval in shape, a reminder to the mourner that he is not alone in his grief. Suffering goes around the whole world. Why eat mourner's food on a festival? Because the first day of Passover always falls on the same day of the week on which Tisha Be-Av (the anniversary of the destruction of the Temple) will fall that year. Hence the connection between mourning and Passover.

12. *Tzafon*: hidden. The *afikoman* is taken from its hiding place and eaten. In many communities, the children hunt for the *afikoman*. When they find it they refuse to surrender it until they are promised a present. Some of the more staid Rabbis tended to frown on this custom, saying tht it encourages children to be mercenary. But the majority have seen nothing wrong in this amusing game of bargaining, which does, after all, help to make the Seder more enjoyable for children. Moreover, it keeps them awake until the end of the meal.

13. *Berakh*: blessing. Grace after meals is recited.

14. *Hallel*: praise. The special hymns of praise in the Book of Psalms, known as Hallel, are sung by all the participants.

15. *Nirtzah*: acceptance. Songs are sung in which God is entreated to accept the service of the Seder. Some of these songs, like *Ḥad Gadya*, are purely folk songs, but with a little imagination one can find significance in them. The little kid, for instance, bleating plaintively until the Seder is over, can represent the Jewish people, which, for all its straying from the path, still survives and will survive until the end of time.

13

Shavuot and Sefirat Ha-Omer

The Feast of Weeks

Scripture states (Leviticus 23:15): "And from the day you bring the sheaf (omer) of wave-offering, you shall count off seven weeks (shavuot)." On the second day of Passover a meal offering was brought to the Temple; it consisted of a sheaf of barley, which was waved by the priest, hence the term "wave-offering." (Strictly speaking, the word omer is the name of a measure. A sheaf having this measure was brought as an offering in thanks for the barley harvest.) Seven weeks were counted from this second day of Passover, and at the end of the seven weeks, on the fiftieth day, a festival was to be celebrated (verse 21). This is Shavuot, "The Feast of Weeks."

Most scholars believe that Shavuot was originally a harvest festival pure and simple. However, a careful reading of Exodus, chapter 19, shows that in the third month (Sivan) there took place the revelation at Sinai. Since the sixth day of Sivan is the date of Shavuot (fifty days after the second day of Passover, the sixteenth day of Nusan) and the date of the Sinaitic revelation coincides, Shavuot came to be a celebration not of the harvest but of the revelation. In the prayers of the day, Shavuot is always referred to as "the season of the giving of our Torah."

This explains why there are no special rituals for Shavuot as there are for Passover and Sukkot. Shavuot, originally, seems to have been an adjunct of Passover, which also seems to have had associations with the harvest. An adjunct festival does not require rituals of its own. Moreover, even when Shavuot became the festival celebrating the giving of the Torah, new rituals expressing this theme were not created. This might well have been because rituals have a particular aim and give expression to a particular theme—freedom on Passover, for example, or trust in God on Sukkot. But there is no need for specific rituals to give expression to Shavuot, since its theme—the giving of the Torah—embraces all others.

Shavuot Customs

Yet, especially in the Middle Ages, Shavuot customs did evolve. It is the custom, for example, to decorate the synagogue with flowers and

The Waving of the Omer

"Rabbi Hiyya bar Abba said in the name of Rabbi Johanan: The omer was waved forward and backward, upward and downward. Forward and backward, that is to Him to whom the four directions belong; upward and downward, that is to Him to whom heaven and earth belong."

(*Babylonian Talmud, Menahot* 62a)

Accepting the Torah Every Day

A Ḥasidic rabbi was asked: "Why do we say in the prayers on Shavuot that it is the season of the giving of the Torah rather than the season of accepting the Torah? After all, the true celebration is because Israel accepted the Torah and promised to keep it." He replied: "The Torah was given at a particular time, but the acceptance of the Torah is not limited to any time or season or place. It has to be accepted each day in a new and fresh way, as if it had just been given."

plants. This is said to represent what happened at Sinai when the Torah was given. Mount Sinai is a barren mountain, but when the Torah was given it became covered with luxuriant plants and fragrant flowers. The Torah brings the fragrance of spirituality into Jewish life.

"There is no need for specific rituals to give expression to Shavuot since its theme—the giving of the Torah—embraces all others."

It is said that barren Mount Sinai became covered with flowers when the Torah was given.

Another custom is to eat dairy dishes on Shavuot. Cheesecake is a favorite. One of the reasons given is that the Torah is like milk. First, because like milk it nourishes young and old. Secondly, milk quickly turns sour if it is left in vessels of the precious metals, gold and silver. The students of the Torah who have golden opinions of themselves, who are arrogant and lack humility, are not true representatives of Jewish learning. They make the Torah seem repellent. They turn its nourishing milk sour.

A custom developed by the mystics of Safed in the sixteenth century, now a universal custom, is to stay up all night on Shavuot studying the Torah. Originally the custom involved studying a sample of all the classical sources of Judaism—passages from the Bible, the Mishnah, the Gemara, the Zohar, and so forth. Many still do this, reading the texts out of an anthology prepared for the purpose called *Tikkun Leyl Shavuot*, "The Arrangement for the Night of Shavuot". But others prefer to devote the time to a study session in which a single topic is examined in depth.

"A custom developed by the mystics of the sixteenth century is to stay up all night on Shavuot studying the Torah."

For many poetic reasons, dairy foods became traditional on Shavuot.

The second day of Shavuot, like that of Passover and Sukkot, is celebrated as a festival outside of Israel, where only one day is observed. Some communities hold a midnight vigil on the second night of Shavuot as well, but on this night the Book of Psalms is read. Why the Book of Psalms? First, because the Book of Ruth is read on Shavuot (it deals with the theme of harvest). Ruth is the ancestor of David, the traditional author of the Book of Psalms. Second, because of the tradition that David died on the day corresponding to the second day of Shavuot. (There was no second day of Shavuot in David's time.) The two heroes of Shavuot are, then, Moses and David, the lawgiver and the psalmist, the teacher and the poet.

Lawgiver and Psalmist

Rabbi A. Amiel has a sermon in which he notes that the two different types of leader represented by Moses, the lawgiver, and David, the psalmist, are found in most periods of Jewish history. For instance, in the Middle Ages there were Maimonides, the rationalist thinker, and Judah Halevi, the poet. In the eighteenth century there were the great legal scholar, the Gaon of Vilna, and the mystical founder of Ḥasidism, the Baal Shem Tov.

Counting the Omer

Rabbinic tradition has it that when the Torah speaks of counting the seven weeks from the second day of Passover to Shavuot, this counting has to be understood quite literally. Each day should be counted: "This is the first day of the Omer"; "this is the second day of the Omer"; "this is the tenth day, which is one week and three days of the Omer," and so on. This practice is known as "counting the Omer," although, as we have seen, it is actually counting *from* the Omer.

Counting the Omer has been interpreted by Jewish thinkers to denote that, after freedom, the theme of Passover, one eagerly counts the days and weeks until the Torah is welcomed on Shavuot. An illustration given is of a slave counting the days to his freedom or, more romantically, of a lover counting the days until he will be united with his beloved.

In the Middle Ages, the Omer period became one of mourning, albeit in a minor key. One of the reasons given is that the disciples of Rabbi Akiba died during this period. It is the practice not to have a haircut during this period, except on certain days. Weddings are also not celebrated, except on certain days permitted by local custom.

Lag Ba-Omer

The word *lag* is formed by the letters *lamed* and *gimmel*, the numerical value of which is *thirty* and *three*. This day, the thirty-third day of the Omer, is a minor festival. The usual reason given is that Rabbi

Simeon bar Yohai, to whom the authorship of the Zohar is attributed, died on this day. The ascent of this saint's soul to Heaven is described as his "wedding," the reunion of his soul with its Source. Weddings are therefore permitted on this day, even though it is during the period of the Omer.

Lag Ba-Omer became a scholar's festival, a celebration of the joy experienced by the students of the Torah. The reason is none too clear, but in many communities the teachers and their pupils would go out into the woods on Lag Ba-Omer to shoot with bows and arrows. Some see in this an echo of the Bar Kochba Revolt against the might of Rome, which took place in the days of Rabbi Simeon bar Yohai, or very near to his period. The origins of some customs are veiled in obscurity.

An Omer calendar from the eighteenth century.

Suppose someone starts a letter with the date: "On the thirtieth day of the Omer." Does this serve as "counting"? The later authorities argue that this depends on a more general question: Does the written word have the full force of a verbal declaration? For instance, does a written oath have the same significance as one that is taken verbally? Opinions differ.

Yom Ha-Atzmaut

The fifth of Iyar, corresponding to the twenty-sixth day of the Omer, is the anniversary of the establishment of the State of Israel—*Yom Ha-Atzmaut* ("Independence Day"). Although this day belongs to the Omer period of mourning, many rabbis hold that it is a festive day, for obvious reasons, and weddings can be celebrated on this day. In many communities, both in and outside of Israel, the Hallel is recited, as it is on a festival, and a special order of service has been introduced. No doubt, as time goes on, this day will find permanent lodging in the Jewish calendar.

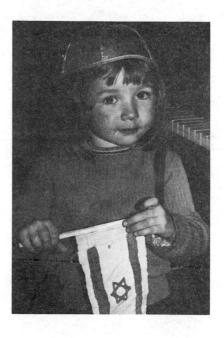

14

Sukkot

Biblical Origins

The two main rituals of the Sukkot festival are the taking in the hand of the four plants and sitting in the *sukkah*. The relevant passage in the Torah for both of these is from Leviticus (23:40 – 43):

On the first day you shall take the fruit of goodly trees, branches of palm trees, boughs of leafy trees, and willows of the brook, and you shall rejoice before the Lord your God seven days. You shall observe it as a festival of the Lord for seven days in the year; you shall observe it in the seventh month as a law for all time throughout the ages. You shall live in booths (*sukkot*) seven days; all citizens in Israel shall dwell in booths. In order that future generations may know that I made the people of Israel live in booths when I brought them out of the land of Egypt, I am the Lord your God.

"You shall live in booths seven days." (Leviticus 23:42) A painting by Marc Chagall.

The Lulav and Etrog

The tradition understands "the fruit of goodly trees" to be the *etrog*; "branches of palm trees" to be the *lulav*; "boughs of leafy trees" to be the *myrtle*; and "willows of the brook," naturally, to be the willow. The procedure is to bind the *lulav* (using strands of the palm) together with three twigs of myrtle to the right and two of willow to the left. The *etrog* is held separately in the left hand; the *lulav*, myrtle, and willow in the right hand. As the most prominent of the four plants, the *lulav* is given the place of honor on the right, and the benediction refers specifically to it: "who has commanded us to take the *lulav*" (that is, the *lulav* and the other three plants).

The *etrog* should be free of spots; it should not be round but should taper to a point. It should not be smooth like a lemon nor should it have ridges. At the bottom of the *etrog* there is a short stem known as the *oketz*; at the top there is a little round point, knob-shaped, known as the *pittem*. The *etrog* must have an unbroken *pittem*.

If only we would examine our souls on Yom Kippur as we examine the *lulav* and *etrog* on Sukkot.

Pittem

The *etrog* must have the knob-shaped *pittem* at the top. If this is broken off the *etrog* cannot be used. If, however, the *etrog* grew without a *pittem* it is fit for use. Where the *etrog* grew with a *pittem* it becomes incomplete if the *pittem* is broken off. But where it never had a *pittem* it is an inferior *etrog*, but still whole, in that it retains all the wholeness it ever had. A lesson: The gifted person who squanders his gifts lacks wholeness. The less gifted person who makes the most of his talents has a whole personality.

The *lulav* should also taper to a point, and its central stem should not be split or cut off at the end. The leaves of the myrtle should be sufficiently thick to cover the stem. All four plants should be fresh, not withered. It is customary to wrap them, when they are not being used, in moist towels or cloths to preserve their freshness, except for the *etrog*, which does not lose its freshness for a long time.

An object used for the performance of a *mitzvah* should, if possible, be used for another *mitzvah*. It used to be the practice, when Passover *matzot* were baked by hand, to heat the oven with the willows left over from Sukkot. Today, on the same principle, some people make a preserve of the *etrog* and enjoy it on Sabbaths succeeding the Sukkot festival.

The Meaning of the Four Plants

Maimonides, in his *Guide for the Perplexed*, understands the command to take the four plants as a means of giving thanks to God for His bounty at the harvest season. Any plants could theoretically have been used for this purpose, but these four only are used because they are fresh and beautiful at this season in the land of Israel. But many teachers, not content with such a prosaic interpretation, have read rather more poetic ideas into the ritual of the four plants. Here are two of the better known: The *etrog* is heartshaped; the *lulav* can represent the backbone; the myrtle looks like the mouth; the willow like the eye. All human faculties are to be used in the service of God. The Jew should have a good heart (kindly and compassionate); a firm backbone (brave and assertive); a good eye (capable of seeing the good in others and looking benevolently at their successes and achievements); and a mouth to speak Jewishly by studying the Torah, praying and offering good counsel to those in need.

Another popular interpretation ascribes to the *etrog* both taste and fragrance; it represents those who have both the nourishing taste of Torah learning and the fragrance of good deeds. The *lulav* has taste (the dates that grow on the palm), but no fragrance. It represents those who are learned but lacking in good deeds. Conversely, the myrtle is fragrant but has no taste. It represents good people with little learning. Finally, the willow has neither taste nor fragrance. It represents those with neither good deeds nor learning. Yet, and this is the point, all four plants must be taken together. It takes all sorts to make a world and all sorts to make a Jewish community. No one must be excluded; there is no one without a contribution to make to the common good.

"As the etrog *is heartshaped, so should a Jew have a good heart; as the* lulav *is like a backbone, so should a Jew be brave and assertive."*

Waving the Lulav

In addition simply to taking the *lulav* in the hand, at certain parts of the service they are held together and waved in all directions. One reason given in the Talmud is that the waving wards off harmful winds. A more figurative interpretation of this same idea is that when God is served with joy, all harmful and hurtful ideas are banished. As we noted earlier, in connection with waving the *omer*, there is also the idea here that God is hailed as the Lord of all directions and above and below, in Heaven and on earth.

The waving is done as follows. First, three times towards the east; then three times to the south; three times to the west; three times to the north; then three time above and three times below. While waving the *lulav* the worshiper faces the east; only the *lulav* is turned toward the other directions, not the worshiper's body and face. When the *lulav* is waved downward the tip should still point up. It must always be held the right side up, the way in which the branches grow from the tree. The downward movement is done simply by pulling the *lulav* downward, not by inverting it.

> *"By waving the* lulav *in all directions, God is hailed as the Lord of all directions, in Heaven and on earth."*

That the four plants are to be held always in the way they grow—upward not downward—has been understood as a hint that the Torah does not wish to thwart human growth but to encourage humans to reach out toward the full development of their personalities.

The *lulav* waving occurs during the *Hallel* section of the festival service. It is waved when the words, "O God save now," are uttered, but not during the words, "O God prosper now." Perhaps the idea here is that before God can help, human beings have to bestir themselves. God helps those who help themselves. But once human efforts have proved successful, those who have made the effort should remain still, thanking God who has made it all possible, as if to say: "My efforts are as nothing without Your help."

The Sukkah

A *sukkah* consists of walls with a covering, the latter known (from the same root as *sukkah*) as the *sekhakh*. The *sukkah* should have at least three walls. (Actually, only two complete walls are required, but since the rules for the construction of the third incomplete wall are extremely complicated it is now the custom to have three complete walls.) The walls need not be solid walls of brick or wood. Any material can be used, such as cardboard or even cloth sheets, provided that these are securely fastened and cannot collapse in the wind.

The *sekhakh* has to be made of things that grow from the soil, but when used for the *sekhakh*, they must be detached from the soil. One can use, for instance, straw or tree branches, but not the leaves and branches of a tree that is growing in the soil by simply fixing the walls underneath these. The *sekhakh* should be fairly thick. As the Talmud puts it, there must be more shade than light, that is, more covering than uncovered spaces. Nevertheless, it is customary to leave the *sekhakh* sufficiently thin here and there so that the stars can be seen through it at night. The *sukkah* should not be put up under a roof or overhanging balcony because then the *sekhakh* is not directly open to the sky. It is incorrect, for instance, for people who live in apartments to erect *sukkah* on the balcony if the floor of the balcony above overhangs it.

Some synagogues build a *sukkah* by converting one of the halls or rooms into such. This is done by having a sliding roof, which can be drawn back to leave a space open to the sky and into which the *sekhakh* can be positioned. There is no point, however, in erecting a *sukkah* in the sanctuary, since the *sukkah* would then be underneath the synagogue roof and invalid as a *sukkah*. Even if the sanctuary roof can be withdrawn, it is still incorrect to place a *sukkah* there, because one may not eat in a synagogue.

The *sukkah* teaches us not to put our trust in the size or strength or improvements of a house, but in the Creator. Illustration from a book printed in 1734.

Hidden Mitzvah

The Rabbis speak of adorning the *mitzvot*, that is, making the objects with which *mitzvot* are performed as attractive and as beautiful as possible. Consequently, the *sukkah* is decorated with hanging fruit, flowers, and other decorations. Many *sukkot* have pictures on the walls. These, say the Rabbis, are dedicated to the *sukkah* for the duration of the festival; one should not take away any of the *sukkah* decorations for use outside the *sukkah* until the festival is over. Many Ḥasidic Rebbes in Galicia would spend enormous amounts of money for the decoration of their *sukkah*. This was not true of the famous master, Rabbi Hayyim Halberstam of Zanz. The Zanzer preferred a sparsely decorated *sukkah*; the money he saved in this way he donated to charity. He used to say: "There is no finer way of decorating the *sukkah* than to see to it that the poor are not hungry."

In talmudic times it was the practice not only to have meals in the *sukkah* but to sleep there as well, the *sukkah* taking the place of the house for all purposes during the festival. But in Western lands, it was argued, to sleep all night in the *sukkah* in the cold weather, which is normal at this season, is to invite a cold or worse illness. If someone has a cold and suffers discomfort from being in the *sukkah*, there is no *mitzvah* to eat there. The *sukkah* is treated like the home; if there is discomfort in one room of the house, one goes into another room where it is more comfortable. For the same reason there is no *mitzvah* of *sukkah* when it is raining.

> *"In talmudic times it was the practice not only to have meals in the* sukkah *but to sleep there as well."*

A Sukkah in the Rain

The Jerusalem Talmud says that anyone who persists in sitting in the *sukkah* when a heavy rain comes in is called a common person, because he appears ignorant of the law that he is exempt and wishes to be more pious than the Torah asks him to be. Despite this injunction, a number of Ḥasidic Rebbes would remain in the *sukkah* throughout a rainstorm. They used to remark: "I shall stay in the *sukkah* even though I will be a common person, since it is worth being called common as long as one stays in the *sukkah*."

The Torah gives as the reason for the *sukkah* that it is a reminder of the Exodus, when the people dwelt in *sukkot* in the wilderness. A further idea is that it betokens faith and trust in God to leave the home and its possessions, albeit symbolically, and to rest secure under the protection of God's sky. A meditation found in the old prayerbooks, recited before entering the *sukkah*, reads:

> *"The* sukkah *is a reminder of the Exodus, when the people dwelt in the wilderness."*

May it be Thy will, O Lord my God and God of my fathers, that Thy Presence be with us. Spread over us the *sukkah* of Thy peace in the merit of the *mitzvah* of the *sukkah* we now carry out in order to unify Thy Name in love and fear. In the merit that I have gone forth from my house to run to perform Thy *mitzvot* let it be counted as if I had wandered far and wide to do Thy will. Cleanse me from my sins. Keep me in life, O Lord, let there flow unto me an abundance of blessing. Give unto the hungry and thirsty the bread and water of faithfulness. And let me have the merit, when I depart this world, to dwell and find shelter under the shadow of Thy wings. Set the seal of pardon for us and allow us to dwell for many days upon the earth in Thy service and in fear of Thee. Blessed art Thou forever. Amen. Amen.

The Ushpizin

A charming Sukkot custom originated among the Kabbalists. This is to invite the *ushpizin* ("guests") to sit in the *sukkah*. Who are these *ushpizin*? They are none other than the seven biblical heroes: Abraham, Isaac, Jacob, Moses, Aaron, Joseph, and David. Abraham is invited to be a guest on the first day, Isaac on the second day, and so on. The past, in this way, becomes the present.

Hoshanah Rabbah, Shemini Atzeret, Simḥat Torah

According to the Talmud the eight days of Sukkot are to be divided into separate festivals. The first seven days are Sukkot proper; the last day (the last two outside Israel where a second day of each of the festivals is observed) is Shemini Atzeret, "The Eighth Day of Assembly." Shemini Atzeret is the festival of culmination, the end of the three festivals of Passover, Shavuot, and Sukkot. Since it falls at the beginning of the rainy season, a prayer for rain (*Geshem*) is recited during the synagogue service.

The seventh day of Sukkot, the day before Shemini Atzeret, is known as Hoshanah Rabbah, "The Great Hoshanah." *Hoshanah* ("Save now") is the prayer asking God "to save" or to help, originally, to spare the people from the famine which can result from a bad harvest. In Temple times, long branches of willows were placed around the altar on this day. In post-talmudic times, down to the present, Hoshanah Rabbah became a judgment day, resembling in some respects Yom Kippur. The liturgy of the day reflects this theme: the reader is dressed in white (as on Yom Kippur), and prayers beginning with the word *Hoshanah* are recited (hence Hoshanah Rabbah, the "great" or lengthy *Hoshanah*. An ancient custom, observed at the end of the service, is to take five willow twigs bound together and beat them on the ground. The origin of this custom is in the talmudic statement that the willows in Temple times were "beaten" on the altar. This probably meant that the willows were so placed around the altar that their heads "beat," or rested, upon it. But eventually, the practice developed of actually beating the willows on the ground until some of their leaves fell off (perhaps to denote the fall of plentiful rain upon the trees).

Simḥat Torah ("Rejoicing of the Law") is of post-talmudic origin. On this day (coinciding with Shemini Atzeret in Israel, but on the ninth day outside Israel), the reading of the Torah is completed and then immediately begins again. The end of Deuteronomy is read so as to complete the annual Torah reading, and then the beginning of Genesis follows. The persons called to the reading of these two choice portions are given the names Ḥatan Torah, "Bridegroom of the Torah," and Ḥatan Bereshit, "Bridegroom of the Beginning." These readers usually invite their fellow congregants to a party in celebration of the event.

> *"On* Simḥat Torah *the annual cycle of reading the entire Torah is completed and then immediately begins again."*

A rabbi once preached a sermon on Simḥat Torah in which he remarked, "It is fine for us to rejoice with the Torah, but we should also try to conduct ourselves so that the Torah rejoices with us.

There is a rabbinic saying that the righteous in the World to Come will dance in procession around the Almighty. This is a mystical representation of a procession around the bimah with the Torah. A procession around the bimah moves in a circle. The circle is finite but unbounded. Similarly, the finite mind of humans cannot hope to grasp the infinitude of God, but nevertheless there is no end to the knowledge humans can have of God and His Torah.

Simḥat Torah procession at the Eliahu Ha-Navi Synagogue, Alexandria, Egypt, in 1959.

Processions

During Sukkot services, there are a number of processions around the *bimah*. On the first six days of the festival, but not on the Sabbath, there is a procession of people carrying the *lulav* and *etrog* while chanting one of the Hoshanah prayers. On *Hoshanah Rabbah* seven circuits of the *bimah* are made, a different Hoshanah prayer recited during each one. And on *Simḥat Torah* all the scrolls are taken from the Ark, at night and also in the morning, and carried in procession around the *bimah*, attended by song and dance and "rejoicing in the Torah."

15
Rosh Hashanah

The Shofar

The central feature of the Rosh Hashanah service is the blowing of the *shofar*. The earliest tradition understood the Scriptural command to sound the *shofar* on Rosh Hashanah to mean that two different musical phrases—*tekiah* and *teruah*—were to be grouped into a larger phrase and repeated three times. The original soundings were:

tekiah teruah tekiah
tekiah teruah tekiah
tekiah teruah tekiah

There was never any doubt regarding the nature of the *tekiah* sound. It was known to be a long, drawn out, uninterrupted blast.

A problem arose, however, concerning the phrase *teruah*. It was known to be a sound of weeping, but weeping can consist of both short broken gasps and high-pitched wailing. So two types of *teruah* sounds developed. The first of these became known as *shevarim*; it consists of three broken sounds. The second sound retained the name *teruah*; it consists of nine very short "sobs." There was uncertainty concerning whether the Scriptural *teruah* means *shevarim* or *teruah* (in the "sobbing" sense) or both together. To make sure that the correct notes were sounded, the third-century Rabbi Abbahu arranged the shofar service so that all three possibilities were taken into account. This arrangement has remained the universal practice.

The whole arrangement now is:

tekiah shevarim teruah tekiah
tekiah shevarim teruah tekiah
tekiah shevarim teruah tekiah
   tekiah shevarim tekiah
   tekiah shevarim tekiah
   tekiah shevarim tekiah
   tekiah teruah tekiah
   tekiah teruah tekiah
   tekiah teruah tekiah-gedolah

> *"One of the blasts of the ram's horn is known as* teruah; *it is known to be a sound of weeping."*

"May you be inscribed for a good year!" A New Year's postcard from pre-World War I Palestine, with messages in Hebrew and Yiddish.

There are thus twelve notes in the first series and nine in each of the others, making a total of thirty blasts in all.

Length of the Notes

The *teruah* sound consists of nine very short "waverings"—〰️. The three *shevarim* sounds are each the length of three of the shorter sounds of the *teruah*. Thus the length of the *teruah* sound as a whole is the same as that of the *shevarim* sound as a whole. There is a further tradition that the *tekiah* has to be at least the same length as the *teruah*. It follows that the *tekiah* in the first set has to be equal to at least eighteen short blasts (nine of the *shevarim* and nine of the *teruah*), while the *tekiah* for the second and third sets need only equal nine short blasts. It is customary to make the final *tekiah* much longer than all the others. This is known as *tekiah gedolah*, the "great tekiah."

It is customary for a member of the congregation (or, usually, the rabbi) to call out each note beforehand so that the one who blows the *shofar*, preoccupied with the blowing, will not sound the wrong note. Further blasts are sounded at the end of each of the three benedictions in the Musaf service, though customs vary as to which sounds are made. Many sound just the four notes *tekiah shevarim teruah tekiah* for each benediction. In many congregations a number of further notes are sounded at different parts of the service to make a total of a hundred notes in all.

Like joyful trumpets sounded at a royal coronation, the *shofar* is blown in recognition of the true kingship of God.

Why is the Shofar Blown on Rosh Hashanah?

Precisely because no reason is given in the Torah for why the *shofar* is blown on Rosh Hashanah, the medieval Jewish teachers exercised their ingenuity in suggesting reasons of their own.

An Interpretation of the Four Shofar Sounds

First there is the uninterrupted *tekiah* sound, expressing confidence to lead a good Jewish life in the year ahead. But life is not quite like that. The *shevarim* and *teruah* sounds denote the doubts and the waverings that will weaken the resolve. Yet there is confidence that God will help. At the end, there is the final *tekiah* of truimph.

Another Interpretation of the Four Shofar Sounds

The broken, wavering notes of *shevarim* and *teruah* represent those plagued with doubts. The straight notes of the *tekiah*, before and after, represent those who are strong in faith. Judaism says to the doubters: "Associate with men and women strong in their faith and your doubts will be resolved; your faith will become stronger."

Maimonides, usually very skillful in giving a rational explanation for seemingly strange laws in the Torah, here simply states that to blow the *shofar* on Rosh Hashanah is a Scriptural injunction, implying that this is a good enough reason to keep it. Even the unfathomable demands of the Torah have to be observed. Yet, Maimonides continues, this commandment does reveal a hint of an important truth. The *shofar* sound strikes awe in the heart. It is an alarm, a call to the spiritually inert to wake up from their slumbers and listen to the call of Judaism.

Saadia Gaon gives no less than ten reasons for the blowing of the *shofar*. One is very colorful. The theme of divine Kingship is found in many passages in the Rosh Hashanah liturgy. It is as if at the beginning of the year God is crowned as King. The *shofar* is blown because trumpets are sounded at a king's coronation.

Yet another reason given is that when the Torah was given at Sinai a great trumpet was sounded, the blare of which became louder and louder (Exodus 19:19). At the beginning of the year, Israel repeats the experience, renewing its allegiance to the Torah.

"The shofar *sound strikes awe in the heart. It is an alarm, a call to wake up."*

Biblical Origins of Rosh Hashanah

The festival we now know as Rosh Hashanah is referred to in Scripture as "The Day of Remembrance." In the Bible, it is said to fall on the first day of the seventh month (that is, counting from the spring month, now called *Nissan*, in which the Exodus took place).

In talmudic times there were a number of periods of Rosh Hashanah ("New Year"), each for a specific purpose. (An analogy to our day would be to call April the New Year for Income Tax.) In the Jewish calendar, *Nissan* is the New Year for counting the months. And according to the Talmud, the first day of the month of Tishri is the New

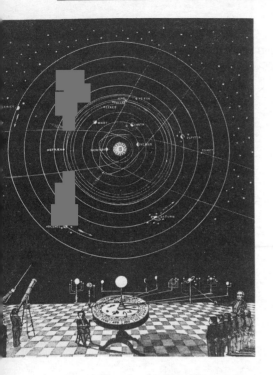

According to a talmudic opinion, Rosh Hashanah is the birthday of the world.

Year for God's judgment of the world. Since Yom Kippur, which falls on the tenth of Tishri, is the day of atonement and pardon, the whole ten-day period from Rosh Hashanah to Yom Kippur became known as the Ten Days of Penitence, the period of deeper reflection on life's meaning and human obligation. Consequently, Rosh Hashanah is unique among the festivals in combining festivity with solemnity. Rosh Hashanah is a festival, with festive meals and an atmosphere of joyousness, yet at the same time it is judgment day, demanding a much more serious mood.

Rosh Hashanah Customs

After the *kiddush,* in the home, on Rosh Hashanah eve, it is the custom to eat a piece of apple dipped in honey, and to recite the prayer for a "good and sweet year." The Jewish teachers discuss whether this practice smacks of magic and superstition. They come to the conclusion that it is not only permitted but should be observed. They make this distinction: Magical practices seek to coerce the powers above to do the magician's bidding. There is no moral quality to the magical act, and the results, baneful or otherwise, flow automatically from it. When the princess eats the magic apple she cannot help but fall asleep. As long as the right words are uttered the spell works and there is no power on heaven and earth to prevent it from working. But God cannot be coerced. His will is supreme. The value and significance of our custom is not that it guarantees a good and sweet year. Rather, it should be understood as psychological preparation for living the kind of life that leads to a good and sweet year.

The World's Birthday

There is an opinion in the talmudic literature that the world was created in Tishri. According to this opinion, Rosh Hashanah is also the New Year for calendar dating. Thus the year 5746 begins on the first day of Tishri and 5747 begins on the first day of Tishri of the following year. This explains why there has been introduced into the Rosh Hashanah liturgy the tremendous theme of creation. God is hailed not only as King but as Creator. As it has been stated, on Rosh Hashanah the birthday of the world is celebrated.

Good and Sweet

The Rosh Hashanah prayer is for a good *and* sweet year. Both are required. The good in itself is not necessarily sweet; the sweet not necessarily good. There are good people whose lives are sour and embittered. There are sweet-natured people who, nevertheless, often fall short of real goodness, tending towards self-indulgence and indolence. The ideal for which the prayer is offered is for the year to be both good *and* sweet.

In many places fish are eaten at the Rosh Hashanah meal, the swarming fish denoting the wish that good deeds should proliferate in the coming year. Nuts are not eaten on Rosh Hashanah because they produce a good deal of phlegm, which will interfere with the chanting of the prayers. Another reason given for not eating nuts is that produced by the method known as *gematria*—the study of the numeric value of Hebrew words based on the numbers represented by every Hebrew letter. The word for nut, *egoz*, has the same numerical value as the word for sin, *ḥet*. (Actually the numerical value of *egoz* is seventeen and that of *ḥet* is eighteen. But a small discrepancy like that does not bother those fond of *gematria*. Simply add, they say, the word *egoz* itself, counting as one, to seventeen and you have eighteen.) This reason for avoiding nuts may seem extremely farfetched, yet there is certainly psychological value in overcoming the temptation to sin by avoiding any reference to sin at the beginning of the year. There are times—the beginning of the year is one of them—when the better way to self-improvement is to accentuate the positive, dwelling on the value of good living rather than on the negative aspects of failure to lead the good life.

> *"There are times when the best way to self-improvement is to acccentuate the positive."*

A Midrash

Why, before Rosh Hashanah, do Jews cut their hair and get new clothes? If someone on trial knows that he faces a merciful judge, he expresses his confidence that he will be able to start anew by presenting a fresh, new appearance. On Rosh Hashanah, we are like repentent transgressors standing confidently before a compassionate, merciful Judge.

Tashlikh at the Pacific Ocean. Venice, California, 1979.

Book of Life

It is customary to greet friends on Rosh Hashanah with the greeting: "May you be inscribed in the Book of Life." From a sophisticated religious viewpoint, this statement does not mean that there is some kind of divine ledger into which God writes down those who are to live and those who are to die. People, by the quality of the lives they lead, inscribe themselves in the Book of Life, deciding whether their lives are to be empty and pointless or wholesome and spiritually adequate.

Tashlikh

The prophet Micah speaks of God casting Israel's sins into the sea: "He will again have compassion upon us; He will subdue our iniquities; and Thou wilt cast (*ve-tashlikh*) all their sins into the depths of the sea" (Micah 7:19). A custom arose, and is still followed by many Jews, of going to a river or brook on the afternoon of Rosh Hashanah and there reciting this verse and other prayers, thus casting away one's sins into the water. Whatever the origin of this custom (and it may have been borne out of magical practices) it has been given a Jewish interpretation. The sins are cast away from the realm that human beings normally inhabit. In all cultures, the sea is the domain of chaos and danger. To cast away sin is to suggest that sinfulness introduces an element of chaos and instability into human life. A very different explanation is to view the sea as the realm of purification, the place in which sin is washed away by the clean, purifying waters.

16

Yom Kippur

The Yom Kippur Mood

Each of the special days in the Jewish calendar has its own specific mood. The Yom Kippur mood is one of solemn awareness of the reality of sin blended with quiet joy in God's readiness to pardon. Like Rosh Hashanah, Yom Kippur is both a *Yom Tov,* ("festival"), and a day of judgment. It is a day of feasting without eating or drinking; the nourishment provided is for the soul. It is a day of prayer and communion with God. It is a day, as the old saying has it, when the Jews are like angels, pure and untainted.

The Fast

Of Yom Kippur, Scripture states: "In the seventh month, on the tenth day of the month, you shall afflict your souls" (Leviticus 16:29). "Souls" in this context means "yourselves"; the command really means "afflict yourselves." Now "affliction" can be of two kinds: positive acts of harm to the self; and negative denial of physical needs. The Talmud records the very ancient tradition that it is the second type that is intended. There is no obligation to engage in self-torture, for instance (in the example given in the Talmud) to sit for hours in the hot sun. The prophet, too, equates affliction with fasting: "wherefore have we fasted and Thou seest not? Wherefore have we afflicted our soul, and Thou takest no knowledge?" (Isaiah 58:3).

> "The Yom Kippur mood is one of solemn awareness of the reality of sin blended with quiet joy in God's readiness to pardon."

Two reasons have been advanced, in addition to that of self-denial, for not wearing leather shoes. First, Moses was told to remove his shoes when he stood on holy ground (Exodus 3:5). On Yom Kippur, in the presence of God, the very ground is sacred. Secondly, leather is obtained only through the killing of an animal. This is allowed, but it is inappropriate on the day in which there is supplication to God whose mercies extend to all His creatures. According to this reason one should not wear a fur coat or a leather jacket on Yom Kippur, but this conclusion does not appear to be drawn since the original reason for not wearing leather shoes—self-denial—was not extended to these. The other two reasons are in the nature of a homiletical flourish without any influence on the law.

Fasting on Yom Kippur (except when to fast would endanger life) involves abstaining from all food and drink throughout the whole night and day. The Rabbis add further that one should abstain from bathing, marital relations, and the wearing of leather shoes (which make walking and standing more comfortable). Apart from these, however, there is no need whatsoever for discomfort. Snuff-taking, for instance, is permitted, as is the use of smelling salts to revive the spirits, and one may sleep in a comfortable bed and sit in an easy chair.

Who is Exempt?

The Talmud declares that the commandment of saving life overrules even the Yom Kippur fast. Persons who are ill are not only exempt from the fast, they are commanded to eat!

Children are also exempt. They can be encouraged to fast for part of the day, adding hours each year until they are able to go the distance.

If a pregnant woman feels an urge to eat, the Rabbis say, someone should whisper "Yom Kippur" in her ear. If she still wants to eat, she should be allowed to do so.

Just Before Kol Nidre

A tale is told of the Ḥassidic rabbi, Levi Yitzchak of Berditchev:

Coming into the synagogue just before Kol Nidre, the rabbi saw nothing but sad, long faces arrayed before him.

"My friends," he said, "why do you look so miserable? Do you think we're in the hands of some petty tyrant? No! We're in the merciful hands of God, the Master of the universe!"

Customs On the Eve of Yom Kippur

The Rabbis of the Talmud state that just as it is a religious obligation to fast on Yom Kippur, it is meritorious to eat well on Yom Kippur eve. There is a twofold reason for this declaration. First, eating a good meal on the eve of Yom Kippur helps one endure the rigors of fasting on the day itself. Secondly, since Yom Kippur is a Yom Tov ("festival") and a festive meal is impossible during the fast, it is held on the eve of the day. Once again we have the unusual blend of festivity and solemnity as the special mood of this season.

During the Middle Ages the custom developed in Germany of performing the rite known as *Kapparot* ("Atonements," from the same root as *Kippur*). The custom involves taking a live rooster and waving it around the head while declaring, "This is my atonement" (*kapparah*). It is then killed and eaten at the festive meal or, better, it is given to the poor. Strong voices of protest against the custom were raised in the Middle Ages, especially by the Spanish Rabbis who declared it to be a pagan custom. Some pious Jews still follow the practice of *Kapparot*. The majority have abandoned the custom, although some prefer to carry it out with a sum of money instead of a rooster, the money being given to charity.

" 'In the seventh month, on the tenth day of the month, you shall afflict your souls' (Leviticus 16:29)."

Whether one uses a live rooster or a sum of money during the ritual of *kapparot,* an essential element is that both are eventually given to the poor.

Two further customs were once widely practiced in the afternoon before Yom Kippur. The first is *malkut* ("flogging"). The beadle administers to each member of the congregation a token flogging as a penance for sin. This custom is hardly ever followed today, even among the most observant. The other custom still has many followers. This is immersion in a *mikveh* as a purification rite in readiness for the especially holy day. This theme of purity is behind the custom of wearing white—the color of purity and mercy—on Yom Kippur. Many men wear the white *kittel,* the shroud with which they will be buried. The reminder of death is a powerful spur to us to repent while there is still time.

Confession of Sin

"The whole point of confession is that remorse is not fully expressed until it is verbalized."

During the services on Yom Kippur the standard confession of sin is repeated a number of times. The formula is stereotyped, following the letters of the alphabet, and it is in the plural: "we have sinned." Each person has particular sins and these should be confessed. It is not so hard to say, "We have sinned." It is far harder to be sufficiently honest to acknowledge, "I have sinned." But the private confession should be recited so as not to be overheard by others. Judaism teaches that an ostentatious display of remorse is to be avoided.

The whole point of confession is that remorse is not fully expressed until it is verbalized. One may *feel* sorry, but still it is necessary to *say*, "I am sorry." These three words, after all, explain what is meant by confession.

It is customary to beat the breast while reciting the confession, because it is the heart, when it yields to the allure of sin, that leads humans astray. Also, the beating of the breast denotes that God accepts the broken heart and the heart responsive to the cry of the oppressed and the unfortunate. It is a way of saying to God, "My confession comes from the heart."

There are sins against God—religious offenses—and there are sins against other persons. Both require repentance, but as the Rabbis

Freud's Story

Freud tells the story of two enemies who were reconciled before Yom Kippur. After Yom Kippur was over one said to the other, "Well, I wish you everything that you wish me." "Starting again already?" the other replied!

Reconciliation—whether between individuals or nations in conflict—is a primary theme of Yom Kippur.

say, God does not forgive offenses against another person until the wrong done to that person has been put right. This is the origin of the custom of people asking each other's forgiveness on the eve of Yom Kippur.

Rabbi Levi Yitzhak of Berditchev once said that if he had the power he would abolish all the fasts except those of Tisha Be-Av and Yom Kippur. These two should remain, for who *can* eat on Tisha Be-Av? And on Yom Kippur, who *wants* to?

At the Termination of Yom Kippur

At the end of the day-long Yom Kippur service, a single blast is blown on the *shofar*. The fast is over, and the festive mood now becomes the dominant one. Pious Jews begin to make preparations for the festival of Sukkot, which will be upon them in a few days. Some, before breaking their fast, drive the first nail into the *sukkah*, proceeding immediately from one *mitzvah* to the performance of another. Although Sukkot really belongs to the other two pilgrim festivals of Passover and Shavuot, the later tradition connects it with Yom Kippur. The Jewish mystics say that Yom Kippur is the time of repentance out of fear, while Sukkot is the time of repentance out of love.

17

Ḥanukkah and Purim

Minor Festivals

Ḥanukkah and Purim are minor festivals. On them all work is permitted. On the Sabbath all manner of work is prohibited; on the festivals (except Yom Kippur, which in this respect is like the Sabbath) work for the preparation of food is permitted, other work prohibited; and on these minor festivals all work is permitted. Since these are, nonetheless, feast days, fasting is not allowed on them.

Ḥanukkah

Ḥanukkah celebrates the victory of the Maccabees over the forces of Antiochus, who attempted to uproot the Jewish religion in the second century BCE. The word Ḥanukkah means "dedication," referring to the rededication of the Temple, which had been polluted by the Syrian armies after the Maccabean victory. Everyone now knows the story, told in the Talmud, how all the oil for use in the menorah had been contaminated except for a small jar with the seal of the High Priest. There was only sufficient oil to last for one night, yet the oil burned miraculously for eight nights, until fresh oil could be obtained. In celebration of the miracle, the Ḥanukkah lights are kindled on all the eight nights of the festival. However, there is a good deal of evidence that Ḥanukkah lights were kindled long before this tale of the oil was told, perhaps because the Maccabees kindled lights in celebration of their victory.

> "The word Ḥanukkah means 'dedication.'"

Kindling the Ḥanukkah Lights

The central feature of Ḥanukkah is the kindling of the lights in the Ḥanukkah menorah, or as it is now often called, the Ḥunakkiah. The word menorah comes from the same root as the word for "light," that is, or. The menorah in the Temple had seven branches; seven lights were kindled each night to burn all night. Since there are eight nights of Ḥanukkah, the Ḥanukkiah has eight branches, one for each night of the festival.

It was considered unfitting to use one of the actual Ḥanukkah lights to kindle the others. Each has its own place in the performance of the *mitzvah* and should not be downgraded, as it were, by *using it*—not even to kindle the other lights. Consequently, the custom developed of having a special light—the *shamash*—to kindle the other lights. This *shamash* is sometimes placed apart from the menorah, but the more general practice is to place it on the menorah, but separate from the other lights.

The Shamash

It is the custom to place the *shamash* higher than the other lights. Perhaps this symbolizes the one whose function it is solely to serve others has a more elevated place in the Jewish scale of values than the persons served, even if the latter are superior in other ways. "They also serve who only stand and wait." (John Milton)

The Source of Light

According to the Rabbis, the windows in the Temple, where the menorah stood, were narrow within and broad without. In ancient times, most windows were simply openings without glass—broad within, to let in the light, and narrow without, to keep out the dust. But God does not need light. He is the Source of light. The windows were shaped in a manner opposite to the custom of the time to show that the Temple was to be a source of spiritual illumination for all the world.

Olive oil was used for kindling the Temple menorah. In order to resemble the Temple procedure, some pious Jews use only olive oil and wicks instead of candles. But the majority of Jews, nowadays, use Ḥanukkah candles. Some rabbinic authorities see no harm in using electric lights, and one sees now and then specially constructed Menorahs operated by electricity.

Strictly speaking it is sufficient for the head of the household to kindle one menorah on behalf of all the family members present. Yet it has long been the custom for each member of the family to have his or her own menorah.

This is the correct way to kindle the Ḥanukkah lights: On the first night one candle is placed at the extreme right end of the menorah. On the second night two candles are placed in the two extreme right branches and so on until, on the eighth night, all the branches of the menorah have candles in them. But the actual kindling of the lights is done from left to right—the candle added, the candle for that night, is kindled first and then the other candles are kindled from left to right. Suppose, for example, it is the fourth night of Ḥanukkah. Four candles are placed in the menorah counting from right to left so that the four branches to the right have candles, the other four do not. The *shamash* is lit and the blessings recited, after which the fourth candle from the right is first lit, then the third from the right, then the second from the right, and, finally, the candle at the extreme right.

The reason for this procedure is that, generally, honor is paid to the right (representing righteousness). For instance, a person called to the reading of the Torah ascends to the *bimah* at the right side. Similarly, pious Jews put on the right shoe and sock first (even in the trivial, there is an opportunity for symbolizing righteousness as important). On the other hand, special honor also has to be paid to the new candle added each night. Moreover, precisely because of the significance of the right, one should work towards it. Consequently, the placing is at the right side of the menorah, the actual kindling is from left to right, and all the requirements are satisfied.

How the Ḥanukkah Lights Are to be Lit

On the fourth night, for example, the four candles are placed at the right-hand side of the menorah, but the actual kindling of the lights is done from left to right—1, 2, 3, and 4. Right in this context refers to the right of the person who is doing the kindling, facing the menorah.

It has long been a custom for each member of the family to have his or her own menorah.

A difference between the candles of Shabbat and those of Hanukkah:

We are commanded to light candles before Shabbat specifically to add light and warmth to the house. But the Ḥanukkah candles are there only to remind us of events long ago. As the Ḥanukkah service states:

"We kindle these lights to mark the marvelous victories and wonderful liberation which Thou didst achieve for our ancestors at this season.... During all the eight days of Ḥanukkah these lights are hallowed; we are not permitted to make ordinary use of them, but only to look at them, so as to give thanks and praise to Thy great name for Thy miracles, Thy wonders and Thy deliverance."

Ḥanukkah lamp, fourteenth century, Germany.

Ḥanukkah Customs

Playing with a *dreidle* is now an established Ḥanukkah custom, especially loved by children. The *dreidle* ("top") has a letter on each of its four sides. These letters—*nun, gimmel, hey, shin*—are the initial letters of *nes gadol hayah sham*: "a great miracle took place there." (In Israel the last letter is *peh*, representing *poh*, "here"; the dreidles read, "a great miracle took place *here*"—that is, in the Land of Israel.) Each letter stands for a move in the game. The letter *nun* stands for the Yiddish *nem*, "take." The player who spins a *nun* pockets the kitty. Although some of the more staid Rabbis frowned on this game as one that encouraged children to gamble, the custom became too well established for their opposition to be heeded. Another idea that has been read into the *dreidle* is that like the spinning top, the fortunes of the Jewish people have varied. Sometimes they have been successful in maintaining their identity, at other times they have been less successful. But come what may they have resolved never to give in; they will come out "on top" of their misfortunes and failures.

"The four letters on the dreidle *are the initials for four Hebrew words meaning: A Great Miracle Happened There."*

The custom of giving children Ḥanukkah *gelt* is of late development. At its beginning it only applied to poor children. Nowadays, probably in reaction to the giving of presents at this season by our Christian neighbors, Ḥanukkah *gelt* or Ḥanukkah presents are given to all children, not only to the poor. Some see no harm in this, but self-respect requires that other customs with their origin in Christian practice should not be followed. It is certainly most undignified for a Jewish home to have a Ḥanukkah tree or for the father to be dressed as "Father Ḥannukah!" (one hears occasionally of this absurdity).

Purim

Purim celebrates the events recorded in the biblical Book of Esther when the Persian Jews were victorious against the schemes of Haman to destroy them.

The central feature of Purim is the reading of the Book of Esther, the *Megillah* ("Scroll").

The Megillah

The word *Megillah* is from a root meaning "to roll," i.e., it is a scroll rolled from one end to the other, unlike a Sefer Torah, which is rolled toward the middle so that there are two separate columns. But since the Book of Esther (chapter nine) refers to itself as a "letter," for the purpose of reading, the Megillah is folded vertically as if it were a long letter.

"The central feature of Purim is the reading of the Book of Esther."

The Megillah has to be written on parchment by a competent scribe. There are detailed rules the scribe must follow, just as he does when writing a Sefer Torah. Although it is advisable to hear the Megillah read in the synagogue, it can be read at home if attendance at the synagogue is not possible. The whole of the Megillah has to be read, not only selections. The reading, consequently, takes some time so that the Yiddish expression for a long, seemingly endless story is *a ganzē megillah,* "a whole megillah."

It is a popular practice for the children in the synagogue to make a loud noise with rattles and the like whenever Haman's name is mentioned. Here, too, a number of rabbis have objected to the practice on the grounds that it interrupts the reading and might encourage vindictiveness among the children. But again the practice has become too deeply rooted to be banned. It can be argued that children, after all, have heroes they admire and villains they hate in their comics and storybooks; Haman is a good candidate against whom the children can give vent to their aggressive instincts in a comparatively harmless way. Judaism, in any event, does not teach that all hatred is bad. If directed against the destroyers it can be a positive force for good.

A *grager* (noisemaker) from early nineteenth-century Russia, used to respond to hearing the name of the wicked Haman when the Book of Esther is read in synagogue.

Purim Customs

In addition to the reading of the Megillah there are three further Purim observances. These are: the sending of presents (*sheloah manot*); giving gifts to the poor (*mattanot la-evyonim*); and having a festive meal (*seudat Purim*).

The sending of presents is defined by the Rabbis to mean the sending (by messenger, which makes it more of a surprise) of food or drink, at least two separate items, to at least one friend. These portions should be of such a nature that they can be enjoyed on Purim itself, not something that will only be enjoyed at a later date. Sending a book, for instance, while admirable, does not fall under the definition of *sheloah manot* as understood by the Rabbis.

Gifts to the poor should be in the form of a sum of money given to at least two poor persons.

The special meal of Purim should be held not the night before but during the day. Ideally it should begin in the late afternoon and continue until nighttime, when Purim has already ended. In this respect, the Purim meal differs from the usual procedure on festivals, on which a festive meal is eaten the night before as well as during the day.

An eighteenth-century *grager* with silver bells.

To Bless Mordecai or Curse Haman?

There is a saying in the Talmud to the effect that one should imbibe so great a quantity of alcoholic drink that one is no longer aware whether one is blessing Mordecai or cursing Haman. This saying bothered many of the later rabbis, who refused to believe that it can ever be right for a Jew to become so drunk that he loses control of himself. They interpreted the saying to mean that one should drink more than usual and fall asleep. A sleeping person cannot tell the difference between blessing Mordecai and cursing Haman. Perhaps hinted at in the saying is the idea that Jews should not dwell overmuch on cursing Haman; they should, rather, bless Mordecai, the loyal Jew, because it was the positive value of Judaism that meant everything to him. Judaism is best defended not by denouncing its enemies, but by remaining loyal to its values and observances.

Another popular Purim activity is the donning of masks and costumes. It is theorized that in this custom Jews were influenced by the Catholic practices at Mardi Gras, which occurs around the same time of year as Purim.

Jewish mystical tradition supplies another explanation, based on the puzzling fact that the Book of Esther never mentions the name of God. Yet the miraculous saving of the Jews could only have been brought about by divine will. It is as if God was working behind the scenes—in disguise, as it were.

Kindergarten children from Baghdad celebrating Purim as it has been done for centuries, by dressing in costumes representing the characters of the Megillah.

Shushan Purim

In Chapter 9 of the Book of Esther we read that the Jews of the provinces won their victory on the fourteenth day of Adar. This is the date of Purim for most Jews. The Jews in the Persian capital of Shushan, however, did not win their victory until the fifteenth day of Adar. Since Shushan had a wall around it, every walled city consequently celebrates Purim on the fifteenth day of Adar, known as Shushan Purim. The Rabbis ask from what date must a city have had a wall in order to qualify as a walled city. And what if it once had a wall but has one no longer? They reply that the early teachers would not have made a Jewish festival depend on the age of a Persian city. Instead of Shushan, therefore, they said that to qualify as a walled city a city must have a wall as old as that of Jerusalem, the holy city. Jerusalem once had a wall dating from the days of Joshua, and even if it now has no wall (except around the old city) the Megillah is read and Purim celebrated on Shushan Purim. To this day, the Jews of Jerusalem celebrate Purim on the fifteenth of Adar, one day later than Jews everywhere else.

18

Fast Days

"*There are several fast days on the Jewish calendar which commemorate calamities that befell the Jewish people.*"

The Public Fasts

All the fasts days in the Jewish calendar are based on historical events. They commemorate calamities that befell the Jewish people in the past. The main public fasts (pious Jews sometimes fast as a penance for their sins, but that is a private matter between them and God) are: the fast of the tenth of Tevet (the anniversary of the breaching of Jerusalem by the enemy, at the time when the First Temple was destroyed); the fast on the third day of Tishri; the Fast of Gedaliah (when Gedaliah, a righteous governor over the people, was slain—II Kings 25:25); the seventeenth of Tammuz (date of various calamities); and the ninth of Av (Tisha Be-Av).

The question often asked is, what purpose is served by fasting and mourning over events long passed? The past cannot be undone, of course, but by recalling past tragedies Jews are fortified to be more loyal to Judaism in the present. It is as if Jews are saying: These terrible things happened long ago and it then seemed as if Judaism would come to an end. In recalling the heroism of those who suffered we will be moved to further the teachings of Judaism, as they did.

The Talmud on the Fast Days

The Talmud states that these fasts (with the exception of Tisha Be-Av) need only be observed at a time when Jews are still being persecuted for their religion. In the messianic age, on the other hand, these fasts will become feasts. Until then, and in periods when there is no persecution, it is entirely optional to observe the fast on these days. Nevertheless, in the Middle Ages, Jews did exercise their option and decided, by a kind of spontaneous consensus, to keep these fast days. In the Shulḥan Arukh, the standard code of Jewish practice, these days are given as obligatory fast days for this reason.

After the establishment of the State of Israel, it was argued in many quarters that the obligation to fast should be relaxed once again. This argument has been advanced even by Orthodox Jews, although the majority of strictly observant Jews still do fast on these days. They hold that any law accepted by the Jewish people and found without dissenting voice in the Codes is binding, whether or not the original reason applies.

A Jew was asked why he did not fast on the Fast of Gedaliah. First, he said, if Gedaliah had not been killed he would hardly be alive today, so why should I fast at his death? Even more to the point, if I had been killed would Gedaliah have fasted?

Tisha Be-Av

Tisha Be-Av, the anniversary of the destruction of both the First and Second Temples and of other terrible events in Jewish history, is in a different category from the other fasts. In ancient times, too, it was treated more severely than the others in that it began at nightfall of the previous evening, unlike the others, which did not begin until daybreak. After the Holocaust many Jews keep Tisha Be-Av as a reminder of the most horrific event in Jewish history.

In the synagogue, the biblical book of Lamentations is read to a mournful tune. Like Yom Kippur, Tisha Be-Av is a day on which there is required abstention from food, drink, bathing, wearing leather shoes, and engaging in marital relations. The *tefillin*, as Israel's pride, are not worn during the morning service. They are, however, put on in the afternoon when, as the day begins it descent into the next night, a note of comfort is introduced.

It is further stated in the Talmud that it is forbidden to study the Torah on Tisha Be-Av! The reason? Because there is no greater joy for the Jew than to study the Torah and joy must be limited on this day of mourning. (For the same reason those mourning the death of a near relative do not study the Torah during the seven days of *shivah*.) Only the ancient Rabbis, with their intense love of learning, could have thought of such a law. For them, the Torah was such a source of acute delight that they held it to be incompatible with a day of sadness. They did permit the study of books with a tragic theme, such as Job and Lamentations, and the reading of talmudic and midrashic passages that describe the destruction of the Temple. Yet even here, because they knew that once the mind has become engaged in a subject it finds joy in the exercise of the intellect, they said that these permitted subjects should not be studied in depth.

"The question is often asked: What purpose is served by fasting and mourning over events long past?"

The "Scroll of Fire," built on the outskirts of Jerusalem as a monument to the martyrs of the Jewish people. By recalling past events, even tragedies, Jews fortify Judaism in the present.

The famed talmudic genius, Rabbi Joseph Rozin of Dvinsk in Latvia, used to study the Torah even on Tisha Be-Av. When he was challenged that it is sinful to study the Torah on Tisha Be-Av, he replied, "Yes, it is a sin and I will no doubt be punished for it. But it is worth being punished for the sake of the Torah!"

Tisha be-Av at the Western Wall in the early years of the twentieth century.

Naḥem

"After the Holocaust many Jews keep Tisha Be-Av as a reminder of the most horrific event in Jewish history."

A Tisha Be-Av prayer found in the old prayer books has been the object of considerable discussion in recent years. This prayer, *Naḥem*, ("comfort"), composed almost two thousand years ago when the Roman legions had laid waste to Jerusalem, entreats God to rebuild the city and restore it to its former glory. How can anyone say this prayer today when Jerusalem is a thriving, beautiful city, constantly thronged with people from all over the globe? A number of contemporary rabbis have suggested that such a prayer for the comfort of Jerusalem should be retained, yet in the name of honesty and integrity, there should be a slight alteration to its wording. Instead of the city "which *is* desolate and in ruins," it should read: "which *was* desolate and in ruins." This seems a sensible suggestion.

The Three Weeks

The three weeks before Tisha Be-Av (starting from the seventeenth of Tammuz) have become a mourning period. Marriages are not celebrated during this period, and many Jews do not listen to music. In many communities there is no eating of meat and no drinking of wine from the first day of Av to Tisha Be-Av, inclusive.

"There is an ancient legend that the Messiah was born on Tisha Be-Av."

There is an ancient legend that the Messiah was born on Tisha Be-Av. The idea behind this legend is that for all the mourning over the tragedies of the past, Jews still have hope in the ultimate victory of justice and righteousness, in the eventual establishment of God's Kingdom upon earth, when all human beings will acknowledge God as Ruler of the universe, war will be banished from the earth, and peace will reign among people everywhere.

19

Prayers and Blessings

Jewish Prayer

Prayer is described in the Talmud as belonging to the highest things in the world. Prayer reaches to the very Heavens. In prayer, human beings are in a direct, personal relationship with God.

The majority of the biblical prayers, and there are many of these scattered throughout its pages, are prayers offered by individuals who pour out their soul in petition, praise, and adoration. But eventually, public prayer in the synagogue became the norm in Jewish life.

Jewish prayer is usually recited in Hebrew—the language of the Bible, the prophets, sages, and poets of Israel. This is not to say that individuals should not offer their particular prayers in the language they normally use, only that normative Jewish prayer is public and in Hebrew.

God's Own Language

An old lady was seen studying Hebrew. "Why did you suddenly decide to learn Hebrew?" she was asked. She replied, "When I go to Heaven I want to be able to speak to God in His own language!"

A little girl prayed regularly for a bicycle, but she never got one. "You see," said her friend, "God does not answer your prayers." "Yes He does," the little girl replied. "He did answer my prayer. His answer was—No."

Chanting

Two further features of Jewish prayer are chanting and the use of gesture. As Judaism sees it, simply to think of prayer is not enough. Thoughts are too vague, too inchoate, to make a deep impression. It is through the verbal formulation of the thoughts and emotions that these acquire concreteness.

Even the verbal expression of prayer is not enough. The traditional modes of chanting the words are, in reality, a kind of commentary, endowing the words with a more profound meaning, suggesting something more than that which can be said in words alone. Apart from the different traditions of chant between Sephardim and Ashkenazim, there are different chants in the traditions of German,

"Prayer reaches to the very Heavens."

Prayer has been likened to a stairway. With each movement of prayer comes the potential for an ascent towards holiness.

"As Judaism sees it, simply to think prayers is not enough."

French, Italian, Lithuanian, and Polish Jews. Even the comparatively new American Jewish community has managed to produce its own type of chant. Moreover, the chants fit the mood of the prayers. The weekday mode of chanting differs from that of the festivals. The latter is more bouyant, more exhilarating; Yom Tov is in the air. The chants for Rosh Hashanah and Yom Kippur are again different: solemn, yearning, supplicatory. It is a pity that in some Westernized communities today, there is little chanting. Declaiming the prayers without chant is more of a Protestant manner of praying than a Jewish one.

Movements and Gestures

There are a number of traditional movements and gestures to be made during various parts of the liturgy. Bowing and prostrating the body in prayer is found in the Bible, but the Talmud, interestingly enough, limits bowing to four stages in the Amidah (the prayer recited silently while standing). These four bows are at the beginning and end of the first benediction, and at the beginning and end of the "thanksgiving," the penultimate benediction. To bow at other places is considered to be an ostentatious display of submission. As a famous rabbi once said to a man who made a parade of his humility, "You are not so great that you need to be so small!"

The correct procedure for bowing is to bend the head and the body from the waist when reciting *"Barukh Atah"* (Blessed art Thou) and then to straighten the head and after it the body so that head and body are in an upright position when saying *"Adonai"* (O Lord). The idea here appears to be that while submission to God is wholly admirable and essential to the religious life, God does not want a complete surrender of human independence. Humans have a part to play in partnership with Him. In biblical times there was total prostration of the body with the face to the ground and arms and legs outstretched. This too was considered unsuitable for any but the greatest saints and is now only done while reciting the Alenu prayer on Rosh Hashanah and Yom Kippur, and while reciting the account of the Temple service (the Avodah) on Yom Kippur. The latter refers to the people in the Temple courtyard prostrating themselves when they heard the High Priest utter the special name of God. The Avodah service is a reenactment of the ancient Temple rites and so we prostrate ourselves as they did.

The Babylonian Talmud on Bowing

An ordinary person bows at the beginning and end of the first benediction (of the Amidah) and at the beginning and end of the penultimate benediction. The High Priest bows at the beginning of each of the benedictions. A king, once he has bowed, does not rise to an upright position until he has completed the whole of the prayer. Rashi comments that the greater the person, the greater the need for submission.

(Berakhot 34b)

Jewish prayer comes with exacting choreography: when to stand, when to sit, when to bend and bow.

A gesture used by many is to cover the eyes with the right hand while reciting the first verse of the Shema: "Hear O Israel, the Lord our God, the Lord is One." This, the Jewish declaration of faith, has to be recited with intense concentration on the meaning of the words. One covers the eyes to keep from looking at objects that distract and interfere with proper concentration. The eyes are directed inward; the self reflects solely on the tremendous theme of God's unity.

Hands

The Jewish mystics advise that at particularly intense moments in prayer the hands should be outstretched towards Heaven. Later masters only allow this if it is done spontaneously. Placing the hands together with the fingers pointed forward is a Christian gesture and is not followed by Jews. Some, however, place the right hand over the left in the way a supplicant does.

Swaying in Prayer

The practice of swaying in prayer (in Yiddish *shocklen*) is quite old. Opinions have been divided on the advisability of the practice. Some teachers were opposed to swaying on grounds of decorum. Prayer, they argued, can be compared to an audience with a king, and one would surely stand perfectly immobile when addressing a king of flesh and blood. Awe in the presence of God ought not to be any less! Other teachers did admit a gentle swaying of the head to and fro as an aid to concentration, but they frowned in vigorous movements of the body. Others, particularly in the Ḥasidic movement, advocated even violent movements and gestures during the prayers.

A verse quoted by the advocates of swaying in prayer is: "All my bones shall say, Lord who is like unto Thee" (Psalm 35:10). The whole of the body ("all my bones") should move and sway in praise of God. The Zohar gives the illustration of a small candle that is drawn towards a great fire. The soul is the "candle of the Lord" and, in its eagerness to be near to its Source, moves the very body to sway. This would account for the forward movement, towards God. But why the backward movement? The answer would seem to be that in every approach to the great mystery of God's being, there has to be both affirmation and recoil: affirmation of the truth that God is, and then recoil from any suggestion that humans can come close to the Reality.

"The soul is the 'candle of the Lord' and, in its eagerness to be near its source, moves the very body to sway in prayer."

Temple and Synagogue

It is sometimes asked why Jews do not use incense in the synagogue as their ancestors once did in the Temple. The answer would appear to be that incense was never used in the synagogue precisely because it was used in the Temple, in order to distinguish the "minor sanctuary" (as the synagogue is called) from the "major sanctuary" (the Temple). For the same reason, it is incorrect to have in the synagogue a seven-branched menorah like the menorah in the Temple. On this basis, many rabbis object to calling a synagogue a "Temple," though in the United States this is a common designation for Reform and some Conservative synagogues.

Covering the Head for Prayer

It is astonishing how much has been written on this subject. There is no doubt that in talmudic times it was held to be a mark of piety to have the head covered. This is because Heaven is described as "up there" (although this has to be understood in a spiritual not a spatial sense). Consequently, the pious person covers his head in awe, creating a barrier betwen himself and "up there" so as not to become overly

The grandeur of many synagogues suggests that when engaged in prayer, one is before the Throne of the Lord.

familiar with the divine. In other words, covering the head is a sign of respect for God.

Even the Vilna Gaon writes that to cover the head for prayer and study of the Torah is not a strict obligation but a saintly practice. Nevertheless, particularly since Christians leave their heads bare in church, it became the established practice for Jews to pray with heads covered. All Orthodox and Conservative Jews cover their heads in the synagogue, as do many Reform Jews.

The Yarmulka

The skullcap, now worn everywhere during prayer and study of the Torah, is for the purpose of covering the head. It is not a sacred object, no more than other head covering is. But many Ḥasidim do wear a *yarmulka* under their ordinary headgear as an extra token of respect for the One "on high." The etymology of the word *yarmulka* is uncertain. A folk etymology gives it as an abbreviation of *yare malka,* "one who fears the King."

Decorum in the Synagogue

Some imagine that a synagogue should be a homely place in which an atmosphere of informality reigns supreme, and some think a small, cozy meeting place for prayer is superior to a large synagogue with hundreds of worshipers. The tradition tells us, on the contrary, that the ideal is a large synagogue where many people worship in a spirit of

"The Vilna Gaon wrote that to cover the head for prayer and study is not a strict obligation but a saintly practice."

complete decorum. The traditional metaphor for synagogue prayer is standing in the presence of a king in his palace. Where a large throng of worshipers are gathered together for the common purpose of prayer, there is the psychological advantage of an extra spur to worship. Human beings are helped by the proximity of others with similar intentions.

There are rules in the tradition regarding decorous conduct in the synagogue. One does not eat or drink there. (This is why a synagogue does not have a *mezuzah*, which is only fixed to the doors of places used for normal living purposes.) Conversation during prayers should be avoided unless it is necessary for the conduct of the service; even then it should be done quietly so as not to disturb others. A synagogue should not be used as a shortcut from one place to another. Even if it lies directly in the path, one should walk around it rather than through it. The Rabbis advise walking quickly to the synagogue, in eagerness to be there, but walking away from it slowly in reluctance to leave.

There are no rules regarding the architectural style of a synagogue. It can be of any shape or size pleasing to the congregation. It should not be built, however, in a way that suggests church influence. Synagogues should not be built with a spire or steeple. The Jewish mystics say that, ideally, a synagogue should have twelve windows, one for each of the twelve tribes of Israel. There are many ways to God, and each tribe has its own window to Heaven.

When praying we imagine ourselves journeying ever closer to the Source. As the old gospel song has it: "Get on board, get on board."

The Prayers of the Day

There are three daily prayers: shaḥarit, the morning prayer; minḥah, the afternoon prayer; and ma'ariv (the Sephardim call this arvit), the evening prayer. The shaḥarit prayer should, if possible, be recited immediately after sunrise, but it can still be recited until midday. Minḥah can be recited from twenty minutes after midday until nightfall. Ma'ariv can be recited at any time during the night until dawn. (Many congregations recite minḥah and ma'ariv together, one after the other. If this is done ma'ariv may be recited even before nightfall, but not too much so; the usual time is about one hour and a quarter before the stars appear at night.)

The central feature of all three prayers of the day is the Amidah ("The Standing Prayer") or the Shemoneh Esrey, ("The Eighteen"), so called because it originally contained eighteen benedictions. It now contains nineteen because a benediction was added at a later date. The Amidah is a silent prayer—the words are voiced, but quietly. It is recited facing east, toward Jerusalem, with the two feet placed together. In the prophetic description of the angels it is said, "and their feet were straight feet" (Ezekiel 1:7); a person in prayer is compared to an angel worshiping God.

The Amidah is arranged in three sets of blessings. First there are three in praise of God. These are followed by eleven blessings of petition, in which God is entreated to grant knowledge, health, and sustenance. Finally, there are three blessings of further praise, the last one of which contains a prayer for peace (shalom). In the talmudic explanation, a royal metaphor is used: first, the subjects praise their king, then they present their petitions, next they gracefully retreat from the king's presence, praising him again for granting their petitions. Following this pattern, it is customary for the worshiper to step back three paces at the end of the Amidah, bowing to the right and left, like a subject leaving the royal presence.

"The Rabbis advise walking quickly to synagogue, in eagerness to be there, but walking away from it slowly in reluctance to leave."

"The Jewish mystics say that ideally a synagogue should have twelve windows, suggesting that there are many paths to God."

The first petition in the Amidah is for knowledge. The Rabbis explain that this must be the first request since without knowledge one would not know how to make a request of God. One would not *know* what really is needed.

Before the Amidah in the shaḥarit and ma'ariv service the Shema is recited together with a number of blessings (the "blessings of the Shema," as they are called). Among them is a blessing praising God for giving the Torah to Israel in love, and a blessing praising Him for creating day and night, darkness and light. For the details of these and all the other prayers, the standard prayer books must be con-

"There is nothing to stop anyone with special individual needs to introduce personal prayers at different times during the service."

sulted. To explain these fully would require discussion beyond the scope of this book. In any event, every Jew should have a prayer book, preferably one with a good commentary.

Although all the various prayers have a standard form (most of them in the plural "grant *us*," rather than the more selfish "grant *me*"), there is nothing to stop anyone with special individual needs to introduce personal prayers at different parts of the Amidah. For instance, if one wished to say a personal prayer for someone who is sick, one could do so during the benediction for healing or after the complete Amidah.

Blessings

"When human beings are about to enjoy God's gifts, they first recite a blessing to acknowledge that these gifts are from Him."

Barukh Atah Adonai—"Blessed art Thou." These words form the beginning of every blessing. (Today many prefer the translation: "Blessed are You," instead of "Thou." Here is not the place to argue for the old-fashioned English form, though much can be said in its favor.) The obvious difficulty is, how can humans bless God? It is God who blesses people. According to many of the Jewish teachers, the words *barukh atah* do not mean that humans bless God, but rather should be translated: "Thou art Blessing," that is, God is the Source of all blessings. This view suggests that when human beings are about to enjoy God's gifts, they first recite a blessing to acknowledge that these gifts are from Him. In this way every event, significant or trivial, is brought to God. Life acquires a religious dimension at every stage.

Blessed art Thou

The Vilna Gaon says boldly that human beings can bless God, even in the conventional use of the term. Just as the soul, in this life, depends on the body, God depends on the world and its creatures if He is to be the God of religion rather than an absent Deity. The soul, in itself, does not need food for its sustenance. Yet the soul does need food, since the body, which houses it, requires nourishment. God, as He is in Himself, has no need for His creatures. Yet since it is His will for there to be creatures whom He can benefit, creatures who require His blessing, then in this sense He too requires to be blessed. This mystical understanding of the matter is more attractive to some minds than the more prosaic translation of *barukh atah* as "Blessed art Thou."

It has been noted that in every blessing there is a switch from the second to the third person. "Blessed art Thou" is followed by "who creates (not "Thou createth") the fruit of the vine." The medieval teachers explained that we begin the blessing by speaking directly to God in the second person. But then, amazed by our audacity, we quickly change to the third person, as if to say, we are privileged to address God as "Thou," but His nature is so far beyond all human comprehension that we must immediately distance ourselves from any suggestion that we really know that which cannot be known. To prevent undue familiarity we change from the second to the third person when addressing Him.

The Various Types of Blessings

There are four types of blessings in Judaism. The first group is blessings to be said when enjoying God's bounty. The Rabbis introduced a number of blessings to be recited before enjoying the good things of life. But instead of a general blessing to cover all types of enjoyment, a specific blessing was introduced for each type of enjoyment. For in-

"In every blessing there is a switch from the second to the third person. We begin by speaking directly to God and then change to the third person, expressing our total awe in His presence."

Ḥasidim are generally fond of drinking whiskey. A Ḥasid who was asked why replied, "When I drink whiskey I can recite the marvellous blessing: 'By whose word all things were brought into being.'" "That is true," his questioner replied, "but why do you have to drink whiskey for this purpose when you can drink water and recite the same blessing?" "Ah," answered the Ḥasid, "if a Jew can rise to the heights of acknowledging that all things are made by God's word, he deserves something stronger than water!"

stance, over bread the blessing is: "Who brings forth bread from the earth"; over wine: "Who creates the fruit of the vine"; over fruit: "Who creates the fruit of the tree"; over vegetables: "Who creates the fruit of the ground." There is, however, a more general blessing covering things for which there is no specific blessing, such as meat, fish, milk, and eggs. This general blessing is: "By whose word all things were brought into being."

Another group is blessings recited before the performance of a *mitzvah*. The form of this blessing is: "Blessed art Thou . . . Who has sanctified us with His commandments and has commanded us to. . . ." This form of blessing denotes that a *mitzvah* is being carried out for the purpose of doing God's will. God is said here to have "sanctified us with His commandments." The *mitzvot* promote holiness and are themselves the means for holy living, the expression of holiness.

A third group contains blessings said on beholding the wonders of nature. A blessing is recited when seeing for the first time—or after thirty days—great seas, lofty mountains, shooting stars, and other similar manifestations of God's creative power. Over thunder the blessing is: "Whose power and might fill the universe." Over lightning it is: "Who performs the act of creation." The sense of wonder at the wondrous world God has brought into being is part of the religious response to life. Belonging to this category of blessing are the blessings on seeing unusual creatures such as giants or dwarfs ("Who has created various

The Jewish response to a scene of natural beauty is to say a blessing praising God's creative power.

A blessing is only recited before the performance of religious obligations, such as *tefillin, mezuzah, tzitzit, matzah, sukkah, shofar.* No blessing is recited before purely ethical *mitzvot,* such as giving charity, honoring parents, or helping others. The reason may be that these latter ought to be spontaneous. The really benevolent person does not give a helping hand to others because God has commanded him to do so. He would be what he is even without a divine command. Furthermore, the ethical *mitzvot* are carried out by non-Jews as well as by Jews. Consequently, when we do them we cannot say: "Who has sanctified *us.*"

types of creatures"); Jews learned in the Torah ("Who has given of His wisdom to those that fear Him"); Gentile sages ("Who has given of His wisdom to flesh and blood"); on seeing a king or queen ("Who has given of His glory to flesh and blood").

Included in a fourth category, blessings of general praise, are the blessing of the *kiddush* on the Sabbath and festivals; the blessings at a wedding, praising God for instituting marriage; and the blessings of the Shema and the Amidah.

20

Duties of the Heart

Duties of Limb and Heart

Generally acknowledged as the most outstanding and influential work of Jewish moralistic literature is *Duties of the Heart* by Bahya Ibn Pakudah. We know very little about Bahya; it is not even certain whether he lived in the eleventh or twelfth century. He was a dayan (a religious judge) in Spain, and was strongly influenced by the Sufis, a mystical order within Islam. (Jewish teachers have never been averse to learning from the devout of other religions where their ideas are compatible with the basic truths of Judaism.)

In his preface to *Duties of the Heart*, Bahya divides Jewish obligations into two categories. The first of these, which he calls "Duties of the Limbs," are the practices of Judaism, the acts a Jew is obliged to perform (discussed in previous chapters of this book). The second category is "Duties of the Heart." Listed in this category are: the love and fear of God; love of neighbor; sincerity in worship; self-scrutiny; the cultivation of a Jewish frame of mind. These *mitzvot* have to do with the inner life of the Jew.

As we have noted, Judaism places a good deal of emphasis on correct behavior, on doing God's will by carrying out certain acts and by refraining from certain others. And yet, Judaism also requires the good character, asking not only that actions be done but also that the one who does them is sincere and wholesome in spirit. The acts should be infused with the vitality that stems from a spirituality of being.

"Judaism requires good character, asking that actions be done with a sincere and wholesome spirit."

Pitfalls in Laying Down Rules

The relationship between thought and action, mind, heart and hand, has been discussed earlier in this book. In this chapter we try to describe how the Jewish masters of spirituality sought to promote inwardness. In this area, of course, it is quite impossible to lay down precise rules. If we are discussing the inner life we must be aware that men and women differ from one another in temperament and disposition. A person's character is never static. It is moved by external events and responds differently in various situations. Furthermore, some of the prescriptions in this matter were given by holy men whose lives were rather one-sided. In their extreme sanctity and humility they sometimes imagined that all human beings shared their spiritual ambitions. The truth is that what was evidently the norm for them is not necessarily the norm for us, and in fact can often be quite abnormal, even in a pejorative sense.

Against Melancholy

Rabbi Moses Sofer, the Ḥatam Sofer, noticed that one of his students was going about in a melancholy frame of mind. When the Rabbi rebuked the student for being so miserable, the student replied that he had been reading a moralistic work and this had brought him face to face with his shortcomings. "If this is the effect the book has on you," the master said, "it is of no use to you. Read books which make demands on you that you can more readily meet."

"The Jewish masters of spirituality sought to promote inwardness."

An example of the problematical nature of some of these saintly attitudes is Bahya's ideal of equanimity, which was adopted centuries later by the Ḥasidim. According to Bahya, it is essential if God is to be truly worshiped, that a person be totally indifferent to the praise and blame of others. The saint is so in love with God that he does not care what others think of him. If he were to be moved by praise or criticism, his motives would become tainted. His mind and heart would not be on God, but on whether his acts would result in the fame he craves or the blame he detests.

The problem with Bahya's ideal is that for most people this attitude of disinterestedness will almost certainly be based not on the love of God, but on an arrogant disdain for the opinion of others. Furthermore, such an attitude can all too easily result in sheer indolence. If a person does good only to satisfy other people, his motivation may not be the best, but at least he tries to satisfy other people. On the other hand, one who aspires to do good only "for the sake of heaven" (in the rabbinic phraseology) is really leaving it up to himself to decide if and when God is satisfied. He may in fact be trying to deflect criticism with the cry: "After all, my motives are for God, and for God alone." God, for such a person, may be all too easily satisfied.

For the Sake of Heaven

The Gerer Rebbe noticed one of his followers declaring, "I am doing this for the sake of Heaven." The Rebbe said, "Yes, but please make sure that your 'for the sake of Heaven' is really for the sake of Heaven."

The views of Bahya and other saintly masters on the ascetic life should be accepted with extreme caution by people with no saintly pretensions. Judaism expects us to behave properly, but there is no *mitzvah* anywhere in the Torah saying: Be a saint. To strive consciously to be a saint is a sure path leading to self-delusion.

There have been Jewish ascetics who denied themselves food and drink, except for the bare minimum required to keep body and soul together; who rarely slept in a comfortable bed; who periodically flogged themselves and engaged in other forms of self-torture. One need not deny the value of abstinence and self-control to see that these ideals, if exercised in these ways, can sometimes lead to (and may even be the result of) morbid self-hatred. It is fine to study even exaggerated accounts of the good life, but a sense of balance is essential when trying to apply them to one's own life.

The Good Character

The good character, as seen by Judaism, is one having the positive traits of humility, compassion, love of mercy, and a sense of justice and truth;

> *"Judaism expects us to behave properly, but there is no mitzvah anywhere in the Torah saying: Be a saint."*

It is in everyday circumstances that one's ability to do God's will is tested.

and one that avoids the negative traits of pride, vanity, cruelty, falsehood, and bad temper. A talmudic saying has it that the Jewish people have three distinguishing marks: they are retiring, compassionate, and benevolent.

There is a good deal of misunderstanding about humility and the sin of pride. To be humble does not mean, as some imagine, that a gifted person should be unaware of his or her talents. It is just as much a distortion of the truth to ignore the qualities one possesses as to delude oneself into thinking one has only imaginary virtues.

Humility is a religious rather than a moral quality: in the presence of God one can only be humble. However, humility has moral implications as well. The religious person sees all intellectual and moral qualities, including his or her own, as gifts from God for which one can claim little credit, except for making use of them properly and that, too, requires divine aid.

There is a religious dimension to the good character with regard to other virtues as well. The pursuit of truth, for example, is not only of value because without truthfulness error and falsehood would proliferate and poison human relationships. If we could never rely on the word of others, social intercourse would be impossible. But, in addition, truth is to be sought because it belongs to the God of truth. Falsehood is a distortion of reality, an affront to God who, as the Rabbis say, has truth as His seal.

Are there any circumstances in which the truth should not be told? It should certainly not be told where the result will have the sole effect of causing someone harm. It is no excuse when making nasty comments about another person to say: "Well, it's true, isn't it?" Nor should one tell truthful things in an insulting way to a person's face. The Rabbis declare that one who shows up another person in public has no share in the World to Come.

"The Rabbis declare that one who insults another person in public has no share in the World to Come."

For the Sake of Peace

The Rabbis state further that it is permitted to tell small, harmless lies for the sake of peace. An example given is Joseph's declaration to his brothers that their father, Jacob, had ordered him to forgive them for the wrong they did to Joseph. Jacob had ordered nothing of the kind; Joseph was telling a lie for the sake of peace. The Rabbis also say that a lie is in order when a person is asked indelicate questions about his married life. He has no obligation to tell the truth in these circumstances. Again, it is permitted to lie about how much Torah learning one has in order to avoid a parade of great accomplishment. Obviously this does not apply to a teacher who is obliged to share his learning with his students. He should not say that he does not know the answer to their questions when he does. That would have the effect of depriving them of the knowledge they seek.

Bad temper is condemned severely by the Rabbis. They liken one who breaks things in a fit of temper to an idolator. Why an idolator?

Because the loss of self-control to such an extent is due to an inadequate sense of God's abiding presence. Even when a parent or teacher has to show disapproval of children who do not behave as they should, they should retain control, making only an outward show of displeasure. Yet here, too, there are gradations. Very few people never fly into a rage. Some people can hardly help themselves because they are quick-tempered.

Ethics of the Fathers puts it this way: The man who is quick to bcome angry but is easily appeased, his virtue outweighs his fault. The man who rarely flies into a rage but when he does so is hard to appease, his fault outweighs his virtue. The man who is quick to be angry and hard to appease is wicked. The man who rarely loses his temper and on the occasions when he does so is easily appeased, that man is a saint. (The Rabbis were sufficiently realistic to appreciate that even a "saint" may sometimes lose his temper.)

> *"Bad temper is condemned severely by the Rabbis."*

Judaism does expect its adherents to be serene and tranquil most of the time. It does not ask them to be "doormats," who allow everyone to trample on them without retaliating. And there is such a thing as righteous indignation. Even our greatest teacher, Moses, is described in the Bible as losing his temper when the occasion demanded it.

The result of love and fear of God is true joy, when the human soul is lifted up and exalted in the nearness of the Creator.

To Love and Fear God

It belongs to the duties of the heart to love and fear God, as Bahya states, but these duties have received various interpretations in the Jewish tradition. In the Bible, the love and fear of God are usually synonymous with righteous conduct. It is not only that justice and righteousness lead to the love and fear of God, but in a sense they *are* the love and fear of God. In the rabbinic literature the love of God generally means love of God's law, the Torah and *mitzvot*; and the fear of God means the avoidance of sin. Among the mystics of the Middle Ages, the love and fear of God is that yearning of the human soul for the nearness of the Creator and its dread and awe at His majesty.

Modern Jews are heirs to all these interpretations. What is most important in this area is that religious feelings should be authentic. It is all too easy to fool oneself. More than one hermit and recluse has avoided the society of his fellows in the belief that he does so out of love for God, whereas ultimately he does so from an aversion for God's creatures.

While duties of the heart are supremely important, so much depends on personal choice and decision that precise, detailed regulations would be more of a hindrance than a help. It might even be questioned whether there can be *any* duties of the heart. The concept of duty implies something a person can control. But how can spontaneous religious emotions be subject to control? The traditional Jewish answer is that the duties of the heart depend on the duties of the limbs and these latter can be controlled and directed. By living the Jewish life in its fullness, by the practice of the *mitzvot*, one can make lasting impression on the inner life. Through action the emotions are stirred, and in turn, the heart moves the limbs to further dedicated action. So the cycle continues, practice leading to belief and belief leading to practice, each a vital component in the total religious way of life that is Judaism.

"Practice leads to belief, and belief leads to practice."

Index

PICTURE CREDITS

The sources for the illustrations in this book are shown below by page number.

1 A. L. Goldman, Photo Researchers, Inc.; *2* JWB; *3* Federation of Allied Jewish Agencies, Philadelphia (FAJA); *5* Israel Government Tourism Administration; *8* Gaston Cohen-Solal, Beth Hatefutsoth (the Nahum Goldmann Museum of the Diaspora) Photo Archive; *10* FAJA; *12* Ike Vern, FAJA; *13* (top) FAJA; (bottom) Eric Hockley, Hebrew Union College-Jewish Institute of Religion Skirball Museum; *15* Malben; *24* FAJA; *26* (top) Israel Consulate General Library; *27* Jewish Community Center of Rhode Island; *29* Robert L. Kern; *31* HUC Skirball Museum; *32* Jewish National Fund; *39* Faige Beer, Beth Hatefutsoth; *41* Warren Solodar, Beth Hatefutsoth; *43* American Jewish Historical Society; *44* David A. Wortman; *45* Union of American Hebrew Congregations (UAHC); *49* Bill Aron; *50* (right) Sandy Castelbaum; (left) Robert A. Kern; *51* Beth Hatefutsoth; *52* Council of Jewish Federations; *53* Allen Reider; *55* Barbara Pfeffer, FAJA; *56* Milton Lubarr; *58* Robert L. Kern; *62* Norman R. Patz; *66* Beth Hatefutsoth; *68* Carmel Berkson, Beth Hatefutsoth; *72* C. W. Van Vlijmen, Beth Hatefutsoth; *74* Israel Government Tourism Administration; *75* FAJA; *77* Feiga Beer, Beth Hatefutsoth; *78* UAHC; *79* Walter Geber, UAHC; *80* Laurence E. Rubin, Beth Hatefutsoth; *84* (top) Beth Hatefutsoth; (middle) Jan Parik, Beth Hatefutsoth; *86* Stanley K. Patz; *89* Marvin Rand, Skirball Museum; *92* H. Bernard Lewis, UAHC; *93* S. Barbara Moore, Caldwell College; *94* Robert L. Kern; *97* Mikhail Makushkin; *99* Robert L. Kern; *103* Scott Weiner, FAJA; *105* Jean Dolen, Beth Hatefutsoth; *108* (top) Beth Hatefutsoth; (bottom) Leslie Starobin, The Picture Cube; *110* American Museum of Natural History; *111* Bill Aron, Photo Researchers, Inc.; *115* 19th century. Beth Hatefutsoth; *116* Robert A. Cumins; *120* Robert L. Kern; *121* Beth Hatefutsoth; *124* Beth Hatefutsoth; *127* Norman R. Patz; *130* David A. Wortman; *134* Mary Lindroth, Caldwell College; *137* Sandy Castelbaum; *141* Robert L. Kern; *143* FAJA